The Secret Life of
Twickenham

The Story of Rugby Union's Iconic Fortress, the Players, Staff and Fans

By Chris Jones

Aurum
Press

First published in Great Britain
2014 by Aurum Press Ltd
74—77 White Lion Street
Islington
London N1 9PF
www.aurumpress.co.uk

This paperback edition first published in 2015 by Aurum Press Ltd

A catalogue record for this book is
available from the British Library.

ISBN 978 1 78131 328 2

EBOOK ISBN 978 1 78131 385 5

1 3 5 7 9 10 8 6 4 2
2015 2017 2019 2018 2016

Typeset in ITC New Baskerville by SX Composing DTP, Rayleigh, Essex
Printed and bound by CPI Group (UK) Ltd, Croydon, CR0 4YY

CONTENTS

Foreword
By Lawrence Dallaglio, OBE

Twickenham has a very special place in my sporting life. I was lucky enough to enjoy considerable success in my favourite stadium with both England and my club London Wasps, and it was always a privilege to walk into the 'home' dressing room and then run out onto a pitch that provided the stage for so many wonderful moments in my career. It is an iconic stadium with a huge history and I like to think that during my time with England we turned it into a fortress. It really did become the second home for Wasps, and because of that it was, and still is, such a very special place.

I first played at Twickenham while a pupil at King's House School in Richmond and I am very happy to recall that I managed to score on my 'debut' on the pitch in a mini-rugby match. The stadium looked very different to the wonderful bowl that we know today, with the old stands on the north, east and west sides providing the backdrop for my first match and the small South Stand looking rather out of place at one end. I was in the old stands as a fan for the 1991 World Cup final when Australia defeated England, and the stadium was a big part of my formative years because we lived in the area and took every opportunity to make the pilgrimage to HQ. My final game for Wasps was also at Twickenham in 2008, when we defeated our great rivals Leicester to win the Premiership title again, in front of a world-record crowd for a club match of 81,600.

Playing at Twickenham almost always brought the best out of Wasps and we won our two Heineken Cups in the stadium in 2004 and 2007, beating the Toulouse Galacticos and then Leicester Tigers, and we won a total of eleven trophies during my time with the club. It always amazed me that a club like Wasps, with a relatively small fan base, could assemble a whole army of supporters when it was a Twickenham final, and half the stadium would be waving yellow flags for us. It was entirely appropriate that when we celebrated the tenth anniversary of that Heineken Cup win over Toulouse in 2014, we staged the dinner at Twickenham, and it was a memorable evening to mark a special time for the club, its players and coaches. It hasn't been just about playing at Twickenham, because the stadium also provided a training base for those of us who lived locally as we prepared for the 2003 Rugby World Cup that we won in Australia. The 'Breakfast Club', which included Jason Leonard, Will

Greenwood and Joe Worsley, used to meet up with Dave Reddin at 6 a.m. each day and he used to 'beast' us in the indoor gym area next to the home changing room.

After ending my playing career at Twickenham, it was natural that the stadium would provide one of the focal points for my charity cycling event, the Dallaglio Cycle Slam, as I finished both mammoth rides at the stadium in 2010 and more recently in June 2014. The Golden Lion was a welcome sight for me and my fellow riders after covering over 2,500km to raise around £1m for the Dallaglio Foundation (*www.dallagliofoundation.com*). Twickenham is home from home for me, and I was so honoured when the Twickenham Experience immortalised the work I now do through the Dallaglio Foundation – using the inspiration and values of rugby to help young people tackle life's challenges – by having them as a major feature of the museum. This book brings to life so many of those images in the museum and explains how the present Twickenham has evolved into one of the world's great sporting arenas. I have been privileged to play a small part in a much bigger Twickenham story, one that is at the heart of English rugby.

Introduction

When Harold Clark was asked to become Twickenham's first clerk of works in 1964 he was ready to walk away from the job as the stadium, in his withering verdict, 'was a tip'. Twickenham Stadium, home of English rugby and the Rugby Football Union that governs the sport in that country, has divided opinion ever since the site was chosen in 1907, and many of the problems identified all those years ago remain, headed by the limited transport links (accentuated by recent decisions to have later kick-offs). Clark did eventually agree to take up his new job and set about dragging the stadium into the modern age by sacking the drunken labourers he found asleep under coats in a converted gents' toilet that served as his office. Today, Twickenham Stadium is an 82,000 all-seater bowl and lies at the financial heart of the Rugby Football Union's £150m business. In fact, it was planned that Twickenham would have a capacity of 125,000 once the new stands had been built, but the 1989 Hillsborough disaster, when ninety-six Liverpool Football Club fans died, saw plans for terrace areas in the entire lower bowl replaced by seating.

It is thanks to men like Clark that what used to be a loss-making relic of a bygone sporting era has been so remarkably transformed without a single penny of government money. The new Wembley Stadium cost nearly £800m, while the Olympic Stadium in Stratford was erected for around £530m, which makes the total spend – to date – of £288m by the RFU to create a modern Twickenham Stadium very good business. It didn't look like that in 1907, after a plot of land twelve miles from Piccadilly Circus was chosen to be the home of English rugby when Billy Williams and William Cail convinced the Union to buy a former market garden for just over £5,500. That was also the year Robert Baden-Powell led the first Scout camp on Brownsea Island against the backdrop of a widespread financial panic that saw the stock market fall by 50 per cent. There were runs on banks and trusts, and a number of companies went out of business. Patently, timing was not one of the RFU's strong points.

It has been a long and sometimes tortuous journey to establish a large modern stadium in southwest London, as the chosen location was quickly engulfed by residential housing and, despite an increasing number of neighbours, the transport problems that made the choice of Twickenham so controversial all those years ago remain. As we will see, there have been numerous attempts to improve the situation, but it would now cost more than a billion pounds to extend the Piccadilly line from Osterley, while improving the road access is a non-starter. Despite these fundamental weaknesses, Twickenham Stadium has not only flourished, it has become an ultra-modern arena capable of staging Rolling Stones concerts for 50,000 fans or Rugby World Cup finals.

The stadium was the focal point for anti-apartheid demonstrations in 1969, with protesters finding a way into the stadium to burn a swastika into the centre of the pitch before England played South Africa. The swastika was never photographed because the incident was hushed up by Harold Clark, who used grass cuttings to hide the damage, and the match went ahead. In recent years, the stadium has provided the backdrop for the RFU's seemingly interminable civil war after the sport went professional in 1995. Not even a Rugby World Cup triumph in 2003 could stop the backbiting, and an undercurrent of discontent remains, with amateur members of the Union still struggling to fully embrace the concept of a professional sport and a professional management at Twickenham. Unlike the swastika incident, the acrimonious rows have been played out in public, something the RFU would never have allowed thirty years ago. Hardly surprising, as until 1986 the RFU telephone number was ex-directory!

Many still view the RFU as a body made up of blazered buffoons who remain convinced Britain has an empire. The truth is very different, and when England stage the 2015

Rugby World Cup the Queen will be greeted by a man who represents the radical changes that have taken place. Jason Leonard, England's most-capped player with 114 appearances at prop for his country, will be the president of the RFU – the ultimate blazer. One of the most often-used quotes about Twickenham is: 'A bomb under the west car park at Twickenham on an international day would end fascism in England for a generation.' This is attributed to both Philip Toynbee and George Orwell, but the sentiment highlights the views of those who populated the stadium in the run-up to the Second World War and does not fit in with the rise of Leonard to the most lauded role in the Union.

Leonard's journey from young player with Barking – where his first-team initiation was to be stripped naked, dropped a mile from the clubhouse and made to run there through the snow to collect his belongings – to become head of the most powerful and richest Union has been ground-breaking. 'I was running between parked cars and darting behind trees hoping no one would see me,' Leonard was quoted as saying in the *Daily Mirror* in 2003.

'Needless to say, a police car drew up and a laughing officer told me an old lady rang 999 when a naked man ran past her window. He gave me his cloak to cover my modesty and drove me back to the club where the least I could do was buy him a drink.' Leonard will host royalty and world leaders in the President's Room at Twickenham Stadium during his year in office, offering anecdotes about the many matches he played at the home of English rugby. He has a wealth of stories to tell, just like the stadium that is his second home.

For the first Twickenham international after the Second World War, each turnstile had to be counted for Entertainment Duty and the figures submitted to the Inland Revenue with tax due. A place in the grandstand cost ten shillings, and bench seats – called ground tickets – five shillings. By the 1950s a stand ticket had risen to one pound, and by the time decimalisation had arrived in the mid-1970s it had rocketed to £3.50. For the 2014 autumn international with New Zealand, the price of tickets ranges from £41 to £101. Despite the increase in ticket prices in recent years, the success of the team – particularly during the reign of Sir Clive Woodward, when the stadium became known as 'Fortress Twickenham' – and the growing popularity of the game in general has meant fans are happy just to get hold of a prized ticket to take one of the seats in the home of English rugby.

Chapter One

Why would you build it there?

It is a question that many people still ask: Why on earth would you build the home of English rugby in Twickenham? In 1907, when the land was bought by the Rugby Football Union for £5,572 12s 6d, after a lengthy search to find a suitable location led by William Cail, the RFU treasurer, and committee member William 'Billy' Williams, the choice of Twickenham was viewed with considerable scepticism by members of the Union, let alone the sporting public. Sold-out England rugby internationals against New Zealand and South Africa at Crystal Palace convinced the fledgling RFU of the financial benefits of owning their own ground. Cail and Williams had agreed to purchase just over ten acres of fruit orchards and market gardens around twelve miles from Piccadilly Circus in an area with poor transport links and on land prone to flooding from the River Crane. Kneller Hall, which had housed the Royal Military School of Music since 1857, was nearby and supporters of the choice of location pointed out that a country position had not harmed the success of the military institution. However, the choice of Twickenham has to be viewed as a major gamble, one dictated by RFU finances which had not yielded as much as had been hoped through Cail's sale of investments. When Cail sold the £6,000 of government consols the RFU had acquired, they produced just £4,919, hardly the kind of return you would have expected from the treasurer of the Union. A lack of available funds was the reason the RFU did not buy the Ivy Bridge site, which appeared a much more attractive option in Twickenham, and instead ended up with around ten acres of the Fairfield Estate, none of which appears to have ever been used as a cabbage patch – the derogatory name given to the new ground. One can only assume that this description resulted from the large body of opinion which believed the Union had ended up with a site lacking the basic requirements for the home of a sport that was enjoying considerable growth in spectator numbers.

While Billy Williams's Cabbage Patch has become the alternative name for Twickenham Stadium, the role of Cail cannot be underestimated in the establishment of a new home for rugby union in England. While Williams knew the Twickenham area well and would end his days at the age of ninety-one in Hampton Wick, a few miles away, Cail was a man of the Northeast. Born in Gateshead in 1849, Cail established the Northern Football Club and also helped introduce rugby to Stuttgart in Germany in 1865, becoming part of a group of players who founded what later became VfB Stuttgart. He was elected president of the RFU in 1892 and treasurer two years later. It was in this role that he would mastermind the move to Twickenham and he found in Williams a willing ally. Williams was a Middlesex cricketer and a rugby referee for twenty-one years, making headlines when he took charge of Surrey's match with the famous 1905 New Zealanders. Williams penalised New Zealand twelve times in the first half for using their detached loose-forward ploy. He would be elected vice-president of the RFU in 1924–25, an honour seen as a 'thank you' for his work on identifying Twickenham and finding the land.

The area chosen by the RFU was first mentioned as 'Tuican hom' and 'Tuiccanham' in a charter of 13 June 704 to cede the area to Waldhere, Bishop of London, 'for the salvation of our souls'. The signatories included Swaefred of Essex, Cenred of Mercia, and Earl Paeogthath. The charter is signed with twelve crosses, suggesting they were early front-row forwards. Excavations have shown settlements in the area dating from the Early Neolithic, possibly Mesolithic periods. Occupation seems to have continued through the Bronze Age, the Iron Age and the Roman period, confirming that Twickenham has always been popular despite being hard to get to!

Twickenham's distance from any area of substantial population around the time of its choice as the RFU's new home had created a unique local industry. The area was used for the manufacture of gunpowder from the eighteenth century on a site between Twickenham and Whitton on the banks of the River Crane, and there were frequent explosions and loss of life. One explosion was felt as far away as Reading, while another is reported to have terrified churchgoers in Isleworth in 1774. Horace Walpole, 4th Earl of Orford, wrote complaining to his friend Henry Seymour Conway, then Lieutenant General of the Ordnance, that all the decorative painted glass had been blown out of his windows at Strawberry Hill. Despite these incidents, the powder mills remained in use for twenty years after Twickenham became the RFU's home, only adding to the view that siting a sporting stadium in the area had been achieved despite a seemingly long list of reasons to have looked elsewhere. Just four years after the gunpowder threat had disappeared, another problem appeared on the horizon to reinforce the view that Twickenham was a rum choice.

There had been other alternatives for the RFU to buying the land in Twickenham, although none of them appear to have been seriously examined. Matches had been played at Crystal Palace to maximise income, with 50,000 watching the 1905 New Zealand team hammer England, although newspaper reports from the time claim that up to 100,000, including the future King George V, watched the match, highlighting why Cail and the RFU wanted a home of their own. Stamford Bridge was one option but Chelsea FC moved into that particular sporting home, while Cail deemed Richmond and Blackheath poor options and even suggested there were question marks over their ability to remain viable bodies. No doubt this verdict still brings a smile to the faces of officials from both clubs who, in 2014, celebrated 150 years of fixtures between two of the oldest rugby clubs in the world.

The decision to opt for Twickenham immediately had the furrowed brows of the doubters even more pronounced when, in 1907, galvanised fencing that had been erected around the pitch was blown down in a gale. The only good news was that the ground had not been swamped during the severe floods in previous weeks. The RFU would have to spend £420 erecting fencing, although cattle and sheep were allowed to graze on the pitch during this period. In 1921 the Varsity Match between Oxford and Cambridge made its Twickenham debut, and in 1926 the first Middlesex Sevens tournament took place at the ground.

Aerial pictures of the stadium in 1927 show the site still largely isolated from the rest of the town, let alone the rest of London. There were barely twenty houses close to the stadium on Whitton Road, and a smattering of dwellings leading up to the ground ensured it maintained a pastoral feel. Just four years later, however, the area would start to dramatically change, with the building of the Mogden Sewage Treatment Works to the north and houses to the south of the stadium.

Mogden is one of the largest sewage works in the UK and was built between 1931 and 1935, covering an area of 120 acres and replacing 28 small sewage treatment facilities as part of the West Middlesex Main Drainage Scheme. The council purchased Mogden Farm after the public objected to the proposed site in Syon Park. The Duke of Northumberland's River was diverted to flow through it as

5

a source of coolant but nothing could be done to prevent the smell from the plant when the wind was in the wrong direction!

It would be wrong to assume the RFU viewed the choice of Twickenham as ending all debate about the best site for their HQ. In 1923 Wembley Stadium was opened by the rugby-loving King George V and later that year a review led by Cail considered the fundamental question: Should the RFU remain at Twickenham? That investigation concluded that the costs of finding a new home were prohibitive and so, having put all their apples (worth £22 10s when sold from the established orchards on the site in 1907) in one basket, they would have to continue with the existing ground.

The last major debate over a possible move came in 1988 with a plan to relocate the home of the game to a site near the M25/M4 junction. There would have been a substantial cost required to find a piece of land for a new stadium, but the RFU would have received an enormous sum for the land they own at Twickenham. However, that didn't come about and rebuilding began on the North Stand so that it would be ready for the 1991 World Cup.

Richard Ankerson, the former RFU ticket officer, remembers: 'I got the feeling at the time the talk of a move was very much a way of putting pressure on the local council. Dudley Wood, the RFU secretary, when the Heathrow rail link was proposed, suggested a circular route from Waterloo taking in Twickenham Stadium, Heathrow and then on to Paddington. The idea was that on non-match days it could be used as a Park and Ride for people heading into London to work.

'On balance I think building the stadium in Twickenham was the right choice but I am not sure the local residents would be as enthusiastic, although anyone who has moved to the area can have no excuses for not knowing there is a stadium close by!'

For the sprinkling of 'locals' who lived near the land purchased by the RFU in 1907, the first indication of just what was being planned for their rural idyll was the building of two stands in 1909. Showing a real lack of imagination, the RFU called them A and B, and they were joined by a South Terrace, an area of the ground that would present problems for decades to come, including overcrowding and failures in the 1960s of the great mass of concrete. The initial demand was for covered stands around 330-feet long facing each other on what would eventually be called the east and west sides of the fledgling stadium.

Of course, the major headache facing the RFU at this time was one that would recur every time they wanted to make substantial changes to the look of the stadium – how are we going to pay for it? The answer was debentures, and while later issues would bring in tens of millions of pounds for purchasing the right to buy tickets at Twickenham, the initial figure required was £10,000. The request came in the form of a letter dated February 1908, sent from the RFU office at 35 Surrey Street, WC, and signed by both Charles Crane, the president, and Cail. The letter, one of the key moments in the Union's history, reads:

Dear Sir,

You are probably aware that the Union has recently purchased about 10 and a quarter acres of land at Twickenham for the formation of a first class football ground at a cost including stamps &c., of over £6,000.

Towards laying out the ground contracts have now been carried out for fencing, clearing, draining and turfing amounting to about £1,250. It may be of interest to state that in spite of the late heavy rainfall the ground is in excellent condition, and there are no signs of water accumulation or flooding.

The Committee propose to erect two covered stands, each 330 feet long, one to seat about 4,000 and to comprise dressing and bath rooms, office, committee, luncheon rooms and kitchen; the other to accommodate about 4,000 seated or nearly double standing, and to have press seats, telegraph office, &c.

Advertisements were issued offering prizes for the most suitable designs and it is found that these, with entrance gates, turnstiles, water supply &c., will cost at least £9,000 more, making a total estimated expenditure of over £16,000. Towards meeting this the Committee have decided to take power to raise £10,000 by First Mortgage Debentures of £50 each bearing interest at 5%, of this it is proposd to issue £8,000 worth and the Committee hope that many Counties and Clubs will invest a part of their funds in this issue.

The Debentures will be a first charge on the ground and floating assets of the Union and will be transferable to any transferee who is a member of a Club belonging to the Union; but the Committee will reserve the option of redeeming any Debenture which the holder proposes to transfer. The

Debentures will provide, as a necessary form, for the repayment of the principal at a future date, probably 12 years; but it is intended to redeem by degrees as and when the funds of the Union allow of this; those to be redeemed being determined by drawings, except in the case of such as may be redeemed under the option above mentioned, and except that the Committee may always redeem as a drawn Debenture, one, the holder of which is dead.

. . . There is between one and two acres of surplus land facing a public road which has been reserved for building sites, and which is proposed to sell as occasion offers or to be let on a building lease. An offer has already been received for a portion of this land with the option of taking the whole, at a price which would make a good profit were it not for certain financial conditions which the Committee, not being a trading body, could not accept.

The surplus revenue of the Union will also be available for the payment off of the Debentures so that the Committee have every hope that they will be able to redeem the whole issue at no very distant date.

Members of the Committee have personally agreed to subscribe for £2,650, thus shewing the faith they have in the value of the security. Three County Committees have already agreed to subscribe £400, £500 and £100 respectively, and others have offered to subscribe for £1,250 making a total of £4,900.

If your Club or Union has any available funds the Committee will be very pleased if you will lay this letter before your Committee, and ask them to consider the advisability of transferring a part at least of their investments to this issue and so assist their Parent Union. Of course the Committee will also be pleased to consider applications from any private persons, but in the event of the issue being oversubscribed preference will be given to Counties and Clubs.

About one half of any amount to be subscribed must be received on July 1st and the balance on September 1st, and interest will accrue on the amounts received as from those dates.

A form of the proposed Debenture can be inspected here during office hours.

The Hon. Treasurer, Mr William Cail, of Newcastle-on-Tyne, will be glad to receive your answer on or before March 9th.

Yours very faithfully,
C.A. Crane (President)
William Cail (Treasurer)

The idea that Debentures would be oversubscribed proved to be wildly optimistic and the call for cash from interested parties barely raised half that amount – less than £6,000 – forcing William Cail to go to the banks for a £6,000 loan. Work on the pitch went ahead and there were enthusiastic suggestions that it would possess a very good drainage system. This appears to have been based on wishful thinking rather than proven expertise, as the heavy soil providing the base – which is still in place under the new hi-tech pitch today – is anything but easy to drain.

There have been suggestions in the past that girders for the new stands went down with the ship carrying them from Glasgow but Michael Rowe, curator of the World Rugby Museum at Twickenham, is unconvinced and has seen nothing substantive in the archives to back this up. Work commenced in 1909 and there remained considerable disquiet about the whole idea of creating a new stadium in what was a very rural location surrounded by country lanes. The *Richmond Herald* quoted the *Daily Mirror*'s 'Touch Judge' on the matter:

> Unless arrangements are come to with the railway authorities, the ground cannot be considered as cheap and easy of access from London and the walk from the platform into the stands, unless one desires to beat some walking records, takes roughly fifteen minutes. I do not like to throw cold water on the affair but cannot help thinking that the rugby union have purchased a costly white elephant. Having missed Stamford Bridge, they should have gone to Richmond.[1]

By October, despite all the negative feelings and comments about Twickenham, the ground was ready to stage the first match between Harlequins, who had signed an agreement (which the club insists is still in place today) to play matches at the stadium for the princely sum of 100 guineas a year, and Richmond. The turf from Whitton Park was too long for many but protecting the surface by allowing it to grow above a player's boots would be one of the aspects of the pitch that would give Twickenham a particular appearance until the 1991 Rugby World Cup final. For that match, the grass was cut much shorter than usual as part of England's dramatic change of plan that would see them try to outplay

---

1 From *Twickenham: The History of the Cathedral of Rugby*, by Ed Harris

the Australians with ball in hand rather than batter them with a pack that was feared throughout the sport. It ended in defeat to the Wallabies and a golden opportunity for captain Will Carling to lift the trophy on home soil was lost. As Nick Farr-Jones, the winning Australian captain, recalled in his authorised biography by Peter FitzSimons: 'On this of all days that growth had been shaved to a height of only one inch – apparently the closest crop ever for a Test match. Perfect. God knows what possessed the Twickenham groundsman to cut the grass.'

Certainly nothing had 'possessed' any of the previous groundsmen to do anything similar for the intervening eighty-two years, and laments about the inability to play fast rugby on a surface that was designed primarily to deal with the wear and tear of Harlequins club matches and to protect against rain and dreaded frost would be a constant background noise from the visitors' changing room. The turf was its usual length when England took on Wales in the first international at Twickenham on 15 January 1910, with royalty joining the great and the good in making their way along the narrow roads or from Twickenham station to the ground, and enough spectators made the journey to both England and Harlequins matches to confirm that money could be made from this new stadium. However, debate still continued about the suitability of the former market garden site, with transport problems still top of the list of reasons why a new venue should be sought.

The opening of Wembley Stadium in 1923 triggered a debate within the RFU, one that would occur again in 1988 about the possibility and financial viability of giving up on Cail and Williams's chosen site and finding pastures new – with a well-drained pitch and transport links that would help rather than hinder those trying to watch England or the Harlequins play rugby union. As happened in 1988, the RFU weighed up the pros and cons and came to the conclusion that having sunk so much capital into the present ground, the daunting expenditure – estimated to be around £100,000 in 1923 – to fund a new stadium could not be countenanced. For those who ran the Union in Twickenham's formative years, the next-best option was another stand, this time erected at the north end of the ground, as the south was already established as a large concrete terrace. Given the problems that would continually be faced with that part of the stadium, it would have saved the Union considerable time and effort to have built the new stand at the southern end. Instead the north was chosen for the new building, with terraces below, creating a look that would remain in place until the massive new North Stand was built for the 1991 Rugby World Cup.

Cail reported in 1924, the year Billy Williams became vice-president of the Union, that before moving to Twickenham, the largest profit they had made from an international was £1,940. At Twickenham they made £5,509 against Scotland, £4,465 against Wales, £3,679 against France and £2,957 against Ireland. In 1925 the new 10,500-capacity North Stand was opened, having been designed by Archibald Leitch, a man synonymous with sporting stadia during this period in Britain. William Cail was involved in discussing the plans with Leitch but his death in November meant others took over to shape the redevelopment of a stadium that, despite all of the transport problems, still proved popular with the sporting public. Cail had been treasurer for thirty years and reportedly died at his home in Newcastle at the age of seventy-six. (Williams, the other founding father of Twickenham, died in his sleep at Hampton Wick in 1951, having reached the ripe old age of ninety-one.)

Two years after the North Stand came an even more dramatic improvement to the east side of the ground, with that stand having a 'double deck' added to increase seating capacity by 5,000, while a new West Stand was completed in 1931, the year Whitton finally got its railway station, to give Twickenham an impressive capacity of 74,000. The West Stand set the RFU back a reported £75,000, but included in the development were new changing rooms and committee rooms – the stadium would retain this appearance until the late 1980s when the North Stand became a real concern. The stadium really was taking on the shape and look that would become so familiar to England teams and visiting players and supporters, and the infrastructure was also being upgraded. This corner of rural England was rapidly being transported into the modern age, and in 1925 mains water was installed rather than relying on a wind pump, while the oil lamps that had hung around the stadium gave way to electric lighting.

What really caught the eye and the imagination was the increased capacity created for the East and West Stands. Rather than demolishing the existing structures, it was decided to fit an extra deck on top of the old stands with the use of support struts that went through the seating in the original stand to support the new roof. Of course, those sitting behind the supporting steel columns had a restricted view, but when the RFU tried to withdraw the sale of these seats, believing fans could not enjoy the match because of the obstruction, they discovered those tickets went as fast as ones with an unrestricted vista of the pitch. Within a short space of time, the 'Twickenham Look' was now in place, with the North Stand, the enlarged East and West Stands with their top decks sitting snugly on top of the original buildings, and the large South Terrace with clock tower and scoreboard.

While the new stands would give the stadium a distinct shape and height, many of the most evocative pictures of Twickenham during the 1920s and 1930s emphasise the southern end of the ground. Here tens of thousands of fans congregated (most wearing hats) to watch the matches, herded into place by stewards with megaphones and being totally unable to leave until the final whistle. The images of Twickenham during its early years appear very similar no matter what year they were taken. This is due to the fact that only one company, Sport & General, was allowed to take photographs at the stadium from 1925 until the 1970s, when they went out of business. At that point, the rest of Fleet Street was allowed in and a far greater range of images would be produced, with messengers given the rolls of film and sent by motorcycle into Fleet Street to make the editions. Nowadays, photographers from around the world are accommodated in the stadium under the North Stand, where they have a working area to allow the transfer of images digitally. It is also possible for photographers to send their best shots from the pitch side. The number allowed around the playing area is strictly controlled as the RFU is aware of the ire from fans whose own view of action is affected by those patrolling the edges of the pitch.

The lost-property office was filled with single gloves lost by supporters, umbrellas mislaid by those expecting bad weather on the walk from the station and pairs of ladies' shoes. The explanation for these was provided by the RAC men who were in charge of parking. They noted that ladies attending matches would change into a pair of shoes to wear to take them across the grass and into the stadium and then put their other pair for the drive home back on when they returned. During this period of expansion in the late 1920s, the troublesome South Terrace had been extended to allow 20,000 spectators, while the new West Stand featured offices for the RFU, who made the ground their home having previously been based in the Strand. In 1937, Middlesex County Council approved a scheme submitted by Twickenham Borough Council to widen Rugby Road due to it being inadequate for traffic, something you could argue is still needed today.

As Wallace Reyburn highlights in his history of Twickenham, in the mid-1970s the South Terrace was part of a standing area at the stadium that constituted 40,000 of the 72,500 capacity, and this way of watching a rugby match – or indeed any sport in Britain at the time – would become a key factor in the forward planning. That is why it was envisaged that Twickenham would have a capacity of 125,000 when it was eventually turned into a bowl, with terracing stretching all around the lower tier of the stadium. However, the 1989 Hillsborough tragedy would change that thinking. For now, it was the southern end of the stadium that focused RFU minds after various remedial works had failed to solve the problem created by years of 'making do' with this huge slab of concrete – a link to the very early days of Twickenham.

Twickenham Stadium would not undergo major building work again until the new South Stand, after considerable debate and planning headaches, was added to the 'Look' in 1981. In 1965, the South Terrace had been closed temporarily due to structural failings, although no international fixtures were affected. It was decided it would be cheaper to build a new stand than to repair the existing one, but planning permission was refused, with local residents succeeding in thwarting the RFU's bid to fix a worrying problem; they would have to wait until 1978 for permission from the planning authorities. Labour housing minister Richard Crossman said in the mid-1960s he would not consider the erection of a South Stand in place of the terrace unless the RFU bought the houses affected on Whitton Road – they would, in total, purchase twenty-two of these over the years, with various staff members living in the accommodation that was accumulated.

During this period of debate over what to do with the 'problem child' of the stadium, the RFU were reminded that a report in 1956 into the structural stability of the South Terrace had predicted that it would last for a maximum of twenty-five years. This information was never revealed to the hundreds of thousands who would enthusiastically take their place on the terracing to cheer on England or their opponents.

One of those who used to watch from the South Terrace was a young Dudley Wood, who would become RFU secretary in 1986 and play such a significant role in creating the modern Twickenham. With rumours of overcrowding and some evidence gleaned by the RFU about what was happening in the terracing areas, most notably the southern end, it was obvious to all that something significant had to be done. Finding ways of funding a new South Stand included a failed scheme to allow ASDA to build a supermarket on stilts in the north car park which allowed cars to be parked underneath. The building of flats also fell foul of the planners and it appeared the RFU was constantly going down blind alleys as they sought a way of funding the new stand.

The design of the South Stand, which would herald the arrival of hospitality boxes at the stadium, was controversial as it was considered to be a 'one size fits all' option. Terry Ward, the architect who created the look of the modern stadium, was very familiar with the design that Twickenham opted for at the start of the 1980s, as it was popular and could be quickly installed, most notably at racecourses. Also included in the development was the Rose Room, a 400-seat banqueting area that would become the focal point for dinners and after-match teas for players, the Union and sponsors. It was also hired out for functions, delivering much-needed income on top of that generated by the twelve hospitality boxes. There was also an area given over to a museum, initially made up of rows of books under the control of Alf Wright, who had been an assistant secretary and spent much of his life at the stadium in various roles. The new South Stand ended the practice of piecemeal development, and with the 1991 Rugby World Cup looming, Twickenham needed to increase capacity to maximise revenue and provide a truly world-class arena for this new tournament which the International Rugby Board had launched in New Zealand in 1987.

Chapter Two

The new North Stand rises and a very different Twickenham shape is born

Dudley Wood, RFU secretary from 1986 until 1996, would be closely involved in the creation of the new stadium, which started with the erection of the huge North Stand – the horseshoe would be complete by the end of his time at the RFU. As Wood said: 'When I arrived at Twickenham, one of the first things I was told was that the old North Stand was, basically, condemned. It was a wooden structure and we realised we had to rebuild the whole stadium and so we started interviewing architects and builders around 1988.' The demolition of the North, East and West Stands removed from the site the blue asbestos sheets that had been such a feature of the stadium look. They had been brought over from Belgium in 1925 and were now unobtainable. The East Stand asbestos sheeting had wire impregnated into it to provide strength and because it didn't pose the kind of health threat of other asbestos products, those demolishing the stands were allowed to let the sheets crash to the ground during the rebuilding.

Inevitably, money for the new North Stand became the major issue and the RFU fell back on the tried and tested debenture scheme to generate the millions that would be required. Although the 1908 attempt by the RFU to raise money in this way failed to reach its £10,000 target, the use of debentures as a means of filling the coffers was already established. Wood remembers the process the RFU went through to identify the right partners to start what was always planned to be a building project that would provide Twickenham with a complete bowl. 'We had a small committee – Tony Hallett, chairman of the RFU's grounds committee, was involved – and we interviewed several architects, and in the end we chose Terry Ward and his firm and then we had to speak to builders.' The choice of Ward would bring into the building 'family' a man who quickly recognised what the Union was looking to achieve and that size really did matter. The initial brief was to produce a stadium capable of holding 125,000 spectators using seats and terrace areas but, as we have noted, the Hillsborough disaster of 1989 had a profound and understandable effect on what was being planned at the home of English rugby. In typical RFU style, the initial discussion in committee about a new Twickenham involved suggestions that someone 'went away and came up with some numbers'.

That person was Hallett, a man who became critical to the way the work was undertaken; his close relationship with Ward would ensure problems were kept under control and flexibility in thinking was always part of their relationship. The Hallett/Ward double act would be appearing at Twickenham on a regular basis throughout the building period and their importance to the project cannot be over-emphasised. Hallett said: 'I was asked to produce a paper on how much building a new bowl stadium would cost and I came up with a figure of £82.5m to complete the bowl. That figure would have been about right if we had finished everything in sequence and not waited ten years to do the South Stand, which then cost double what everything else cost. Because of the Taylor Report and Hillsborough, we were not going to have 125,000 with a mixture of sitting and standing fans, and changes had to be made as we were going along.'

As the architect charged with overseeing the redevelopment, Ward would be involved with the RFU and Twickenham Stadium over a period stretching from 1988 until the completion of the South Stand in 2006. Twickenham, in Ward's words, had been 'in aspic' for a long period before his radically different look for the stadium was presented to the relevant committees. Not only is he understandably proud of what has been achieved, Ward is also bullish about the stadium and how much it eventually cost – even with the wait to complete the South Stand area. 'The whole of Twickenham, including the new South Stand, cost between

£270m and £300m to build and create an 82,000-capacity venue. In my opinion, it's probably the best-value stadium in the country and if you built Twickenham now from scratch, you would be talking around £500m. It is incredible to recognise that the RFU built the stadium without a single penny from the government – that is a remarkable achievement.'

The North Stand, given the state of the original building, was always designed to be the first piece of the jigsaw; throughout its life the place had looked rather shabby and forgotten. For many years, netting was used to keep the unwary out of the areas underneath the stand where unwanted items, broken machinery and anything that the ground staff wanted to dump was placed. Harold Clark took steps to turn that forgotten area into a multitude of workshops where the staff could ensure the stadium kept operating at the standard he demanded, but even with those positive changes, everyone accepted the North Stand had served its purpose and it was time for change. Ward remembers the economic climate that existed in Britain, and more importantly London, at that time. 'The North Stand was built for about £16m and it was 18,000 capacity, but we were competing with Docklands at that time and men and materials were being sucked into that development, which meant tender prices were quite high.'

Ward had come on board in 1988 – three years before the Rugby World Cup was due to be staged in England, with the final at Twickenham – after the interviews with the RFU resulted in the company he was then at being awarded the contract: 'At that time, I was working for Husband & Co in

Sheffield and we were interviewed as one of five competing for the contract with the RFU. There weren't that many practices doing sports stadia – it was a select group – we had done the first cantilevered stand in the country at Hillsborough in 1962 and also the Nottingham Forest ground and we won the "beauty parade" to do Twickenham. The first meeting with the RFU was in June 1988 and while it was specifically for the new North Stand, we were asked to design the North Stand so that it could be taken around and the stadium could ultimately become a bowl. Brian Savage was the chairman of the RFU grounds committee and, after one of the other members died, Tony Hallett came on board to join the working party. Tony and I would work closely together for many years while the stadium was being built. Dudley Wood was on the steering group along with John Clark, the clerk of works. It was fascinating because we had long and productive meetings with the RFU and they acted much quicker than some of our blue-chip hi-tech clients because they had a vision and wanted it to happen.'

The initial examinations of the existing Twickenham Stadium were an eye-opener for Ward and his colleagues. They found working practices at the ground that appeared to be stuck in the 1930s, with little sign that anything was going to change very soon – unless a new stadium was built. Everything was operating to an established way of doing things and this included the water system at a stadium that was empty far too often to be financially viable to the RFU. 'We had a good look around the old stadium in 1988 and in effect what was being planned was taking Twickenham from one era to another,' said Ward. 'There wasn't any heating in

23

the stadium at that point and they used to come in on match days and switch the water on, and when everything was finished, they would drain the pipes and switch everything off again because not many matches were being played. It took us back to another generation and we changed all that by putting covers on the pipes to lag them which meant the taps could be left on.

'The matches always kicked off early to ensure there was still light because there weren't any floodlights. When we started to design the North Stand we were asked by the BBC to ensure that the lights from the hospitality boxes that were going to be built did not distort the TV pictures by allowing light to be seen by the cameras. To solve this, we installed an override switch that meant we could control the lights in the boxes in case someone forgot and turned on their lights during an international match. There were a lot of things in the stadium that were past their sell-by date, which had a lot of charm and were part of people's memories, but we were tasked with producing a new North Stand that had to be finished and working properly in time for the 1991 Rugby World Cup. We needed it ready a season before the tournament to iron out any problems.'

With the RFU intent on maximising income by having as many spectators in the new stadium as possible, Ward was asked to come up with a model that satisfied all of the demands of the people paying the multi-million pound bills. The end game was always intended to produce a bowl at Twickenham, even though that would have an impact on the pitch – as groundsmen all over the sporting world had discovered. The flow of air and the amount of natural sunlight that can reach the pitch is absolutely critical to the well-being of the grass, and Ward would have to come up with some special innovations to provide answers to these difficult and incredibly important questions before he finally completed his mission at Twickenham.

'The RFU said that, ultimately, the stadium would be in the round with as many spectators – as big a capacity – as you can get. We designed it with three tiers in such a way that in the upper tier the fans didn't feel too far away, which some supporters do at the new Wembley. We had to go high to ensure this happened and I remember telling the committee in September 1988 that to achieve what they wanted we would have to build the first three-tier stadium in this country and made it clear to the committee members by stating: "You do realise the highest seat will be exactly one-hundred feet off the ground?" I asked if they were willing for spectators to be sitting that high up in the stands. There was some mumbling as the chairman looked around the room and then he came to Tony Hallett, who was still in the Royal Navy at that point. Hallett said, "We are big men doing a big job, we should go for it," and the plan was carried.

'The initial idea was for spectator terracing at the bottom of the North Stand because they wanted to keep the same atmosphere that had been created in the old stand. But while we were out to tender early in 1989, the Hillsborough disaster happened in April when ninety-six Liverpool supporters were killed as a result of the terracing at the stadium in Sheffield. It became apparent that because people were standing in pens on the terraces, this was one of the major reasons for the disaster. Our plans for terracing included the ability for the areas to be converted to seating if the RFU ever wanted to do that in the future. If it hadn't been for Hillsborough, the capacity of Twickenham would now be 125,000 with terracing all around the lower tier. That was the original design, but we switched to the alternative design which had seats in every tier.'

The Taylor Report into the Hillsborough tragedy came out as an interim report in August 1989, with the full findings published in January the following year. While the report was being compiled Ward and the RFU had to try to anticipate the recommendations that would eventually call for all ticketed spectators to have seating, and major stadia to be all-seater. With the haunting images of Liverpool fans being carried away on advertising hoarding because ambulances couldn't get easy access to the pitch surround in his mind, Ward amended the plans for Twickenham to ensure this would never be a problem at the stadium. 'We had to anticipate the safety features we thought would be recommended [in the report]. The RFU immediately decided that we would go to all-seater and I deliberately allowed for a six-metre area in front of the lower tier to accommodate ambulances, and we had to go back that far to allow the fans in the upper tier to have the correct sight lines to the touchline from where they were sitting. We assured the RFU there would be a minimum capacity for Twickenham during the building work. The North Stand came into use at the lower level for the All Blacks in November 1989 and we kept going.'

The size of the stand and the roof that was designed to

provide the look that would make Twickenham so distinctive required significant foundations to be dug. When they eventually found the water table, the builders were amazed to discover it was tidal, thanks to the nearby River Thames. Ward added, 'We put the piles down twenty-five metres into the ground and it was clay and then gravel. It is a 39-metre cantilevered roof and needed that kind of support to make sure it stayed where it was. There were big soldier columns that took all the force into the ground and the deep piles made sure they stayed there. When finished, it did look, at that point, a bit incongruous because you had this new North Stand alongside the smaller East and West Stands from the 1920s and 30s and then the modern one at the south end. We put around thirty hospitality boxes in the North and that generated income for the RFU, which was very important with costs that were being incurred during the rebuilding.'

When the RFU were seeking permission for the North Stand to be rebuilt, the local council insisted on increased parking for the larger capacity. The best option was to purchase the Rosebine Avenue site that now plays such a crucial role in the overall parking plan for the stadium. Then when the new North Stand was complete the RFU tried to win over the locals by announcing that they would make new television aerials available free of charge to residents, as it was feared the metal in the large structure would cause interference. This did not prove to be necessary, as a booster was placed on the top of the North Stand to negate any of the expected problems.

The North Stand appears – it would be hard to miss it

– in all the pictures of the 1991 Rugby World Cup because its sheer size dwarfed the rest of the arena. It did give the RFU and the spectators an idea of just how big the planned new stadium was going to be, and there was disquiet that the finished bowl would be just too big and the fans too far away from the action. This was a theme picked up by Dudley Wood, who admitted: 'We used to say that people who were in the very top of the North Stand, if they got bored with our match, could watch the Harlequins play over at the Stoop. It was a huge stand and the capacity when I arrived was 64,000, with 18,000 standing, and I remember having a discussion about having a standing area included in the new North Stand to help the atmosphere. But then Hillsborough happened and we gave that idea up and it had to be all-seater.

'We finished the North Stand and Mowlem's presented their bill and it was somewhere around two-million pounds more than agreed and I objected. They said we had changed our minds about some aspects of the build and that it had cost extra money, to which I replied that we had three other stands to build and would they like to reconsider, and they did modify the bill by about a million pounds.

'The stand was paid for by debentures and they were critical to what we were planning as, even though inter-national matches sold out, as a Union we didn't have a lot of money. We did apply for government funding and were turned down, which I was quite pleased about. Once they give you money then they believe they have an influence, and it did come up in the House of Commons with an MP asking how much money they give to the RFU and the reply was "nothing". It meant we didn't have to depend on anyone because we funded the building ourselves.'

After the 1992 Five Nations Championship had been completed, the stadium saw the development of the new East Stand and, following that, the West Stand. It meant that by 1995 the stadium horseshoe was completed to accommodate 75,000 people in an all-seater environment – the new 'Twickenham Look' that would remain the vista until the South Stand was added had been established. While the North Stand had been built during a period of incredible expansion in Docklands, the East and West Stands were constructed at a time when the industry was experiencing an understandable dip in fortunes. Given the battle to raise funds, this was a welcome scenario for the RFU who, driven on by Hallett, were determined to create a new stadium for a new era. The success of the 1991 Rugby World Cup had given the sport a new profile and hinted at the future direction and impact of the game on the world sporting stage.

Tony Hallett was educated at Ipswich School and Britannia Royal Naval College. In a thirty-year career in the Royal Navy, where he served on aircraft carriers, at the Ministry of Defence and on the Commander-in-Chief Fleet staff during the Falklands and First Gulf War, he rose to the rank of captain. He retired from the Navy in order to take up the role of RFU secretary, after Dudley Wood, and while this period would be a largely frustrating one for him, the transformation of the stadium was, in total contrast, a period when he enjoyed himself enormously.

The new East Stand included the press box, an area only

those with accreditation ever see, except for a small number of RFU officials. Hallett had an excellent working relationship with the media but when it came to the new East Stand there would be long-running battles over the siting of the press box. Previously, it had been in the lower East Stand level, with rows of benches and seats cordoned off from the rest of the area and steps leading down to a small bar area, telephones and working room. Now, in the grand scheme of things, the press were to be given a position in the middle tier of the new stand. Having been involved, as chairman of the Rugby Union Writers' Club at that time, in long negotiations over the new box, I remember the seemingly endless running battle to make the governing body understand that placing rows of rugby journalists at the back of the middle tier in the comparative gloom that exists as the area narrows was a non-starter. Yes, it would put them within easy reach of the two large work rooms, lounge area and catering facilities, but what kind of view would the world's media get of the match? The stumbling block was created by the need to fund the building work, and the obvious site for a press box had been sold to debenture holders. What followed was a long period of discussions before Hallett finally got agreement – after much arm-twisting – for the debenture holders to move from their prime site on the halfway line to nearer the 22-metre lines.

The press box was installed and only one problem remained – and remains to this day – how do the rugby writers actually get from their working rooms to their seats when the rest of the tier is trying to get to their allocated seats? While the sight lines from the box help the media to accurately reflect what has gone on during a match, getting into the seats involves either forcing your way past or stepping over colleagues, as you can only enter by either end of the long benches. Power points and televisions are provided to help the media do their job but the writers have to wait until the majority of the stand has dispersed before attempting to climb back up the steep stairs to their working area. Twickenham is not alone in getting this most basic of requirements for the press wrong. The US Open tennis championships are staged at Flushing Meadows in the Queens district of New York, and the final takes place in the biggest stadium in the sport – the Arthur Ashe Stadium. It is imposing, very tall and looks stunning from a distance. The only problem for the world's tennis media is that they forgot to build a press box! At least Hallett ensured there were seats on the halfway line of the middle tier of the East Stand, even if it was the result of a compromise that doesn't really work for either side.

However, the East Stand quickly became a popular ticket to buy even if the basic infrastructure of the area was lacking due to costs. Ward explained: 'When we came to do the East Stand in 1992 there was a recession on and we were able to build a 25,000-capacity stand as a shell for £12.5m. We did a copy of that on the west side for £15m in 1994 and the fit-out of that stand was about £8m. The RFU thought they were quite big bills at that time and they were. Hallett had taken charge of the West Stand and one of the main things we did in 1995 was put in floodlights, which were housed on the east and west sides. It was one of the first shadowless-lit stadia in this country. It was never intended to do the East Stand so quickly after the North but they immediately went for it and it was built in 1992. However, the RFU couldn't afford to fit it out and it was, basically, a shell. We built three tiers, put in plastic seats and some bars, plus toilets, and a roof was put on – but that was it. It was two or three years later before it was finally fitted out. We started designing the West Stand in 1994 and this time we fitted out the lower tier because it included six changing rooms, referees room, gymnasium, medical and dentist rooms. There were also the President's Room, the Council Room and members' area plus the Spirit of Rugby restaurant.'

While the East Stand had to wait to be given its 'whistles and bells' fit-out, it did have a royal opening when the Queen declared it ready for use on 19 March 1994 before England played Wales. The old West Stand was demolished that summer. 'We have shown we can build a stand to time and to budget,' enthused Hallett, who would become acting CEO while he was the secretary of the Union during one of its most turbulent periods, following the building of the stands. 'We have built the East Stand in fourteen weeks less than it took to build the smaller North Stand. That is a very good launching-pad for progress, to get on with the West.'

The East Stand was chosen as the home of the sculpture produced for the RFU by the singer and entertainer Tommy Steele, a fan of the sport, who wanted to give something personal to enhance the stadium. His sculpture 'Union' is fixed to the back of the East Stand near the World Rugby Museum, which has become such a successful and popular attraction on site under the leadership of curator Michael Rowe. Stadium tours are arranged from the museum, and its interactive show gives visitors an excellent understanding of how the sport was born and the journey that has brought it to its current status. Guides take visitors around the ground, imparting knowledge and stories to bring the concrete and steel to life, while the museum archives enable research to be undertaken using carefully collated documents stretching back to the very start of the RFU. The World Rugby Museum was formerly opened as 'The Museum of Rugby' in 1996, changing its name in 2007. Its collection comprises over 24,000 pieces of rugby memorabilia, boots, balls, jerseys, programmes, match-tickets, books and assorted paraphernalia. The Wall of Fame was opened by Martin Johnson, England's 2003 World Cup-winning captain, on 3 June 2005. It is a celebration of the best players from all over the world to have played at Twickenham Stadium and there are strict criteria to be met to gain a place on the wall. A player must have appeared in a full international, have to be retired from the international game, to have achieved 'greatness' in their international career and to have played a part in a memorable match at Twickenham. As well as the wall in the museum, the players are remembered on blue plaques that are to be found on walls around the stadium.

While the East Stand was, basically, a shell, the West had to be up and running in pristine condition because it was the real hub of the entire stadium. With the RFU Committee areas and Royal Box at the top of the 'to fit out' list, there was never any chance that, like the East, it would have to wait until enough money was available to add those finishing touches. Instead, the West was produced one completed tier at a time, with the six changing rooms being constructed to finally provide Twickenham with enough space for more than two teams to prepare for combat in comfort. The enhanced medical and dental facilities allowed the on-duty medical staff – a local doctor is always in the tunnel to stitch up the damaged and to give expert first-hand medical analysis of the injured – to work in a professional environment. The gymnasium, which would become the focal point for a host of international players who lived locally, would stage early morning sessions under fitness guru Dave Reddin, who would help make England the fittest team in the sport leading up to the 2003 World Cup triumph. Today, the gym is one of the most impressively equipped areas of its type in world rugby, with every body crunching weight carrying the Red Rose emblem. The facilities enable injured players involved with England teams at all levels – men's and women's – to be fitness tested, guided through specialist rehabilitation after serious injury and given extensive warm-up and warm-down areas before and after matches. The walls are covered with motivational slogans and the Red Rose dominates an area that also enables players to undertake short sprint work.

Above the gym is a balcony that leads to the Spirit of Rugby, where post-match events take place, and also to the press-conference room which has its own bar – not open during matches! The press-conference rooms have been moved all over the West Stand before, during and after the rebuilding of the stadium as the RFU sought to fit the media into whatever available space could be found (without, it appeared, too much cost to the governing body). There is now Wi-Fi available in the stadium to aid all communication requirements, although getting a mobile phone signal after an England win is troublesome with so many fans wanting to tell family and friends, 'I was there'.

The completion of the West Stand gave the stadium a dramatically impressive entrance directly behind the Rowland Hill Gates, while the RFU offices were created in Rugby House, across the road from the back of the East Stand, and staff would remain there until the 'new' Rugby House was completed in the rebuilt South Stand. The building would feature regularly in live television coverage of the ongoing internal battle for control of the RFU, including the departure in 2004 of Sir Clive Woodward after he failed to get backing for his vision of how English rugby should move forward after the World Cup triumph. When the RFU moved out, the old Rugby House became the headquarters for the organisers of the 2015 Rugby World Cup in England.

With the horseshoe now in place, Ward and Hallett could justly feel proud of what had been achieved in such a short space of time. It was the Duke of Edinburgh who had the job of opening this stand containing 25,000 seats – including his own as one of fifteen in the front row of the Royal Box – on 16 December 1995 before England easily defeated Samoa. It was a successful end to a tumultuous year in the sport as the game had gone 'open' in the August following South Africa's triumph in the World Cup they had hosted. It would be a tournament that provided one of the iconic images of the sport, with President Nelson Mandela appearing at the final to hand over the trophy wearing the No. 6 Springbok jersey of captain Francois Pienaar. The final in Johannesburg against New Zealand was preceded by a low fly-past by a South African Airways 747 which made the stadium shake.

For those veterans of international matches at Twickenham, an aircraft crossing over the national stadium was so regular it was hardly worth glancing skywards!

Ward was able to reflect on a job well done and it became a case of waiting to discover when the South Stand development, the most complicated of all the projects at Twickenham, would be given the green light. On 12 October 1996, in a rare moment of calm reflection during the period that had seen three stands demolished and a new horseshoe look installed at the stadium, Ward headed up to the roof. He walked along the railings until he reached the end of the West Stand. To his left and below was the small, totally out of place South Stand and in front of him an amazing view. Having played a significant role in heralding the dawn of a new Twickenham Stadium era, Ward had taken up this position to witness an eclipse of the sun that dimmed the whole area.

When permission was obtained to start on the final piece of the stadium jigsaw – putting the South Stand in place to complete the bowl effect – the problem of getting rid of the small and not particularly liked old stand that had been erected in 1981 had to be addressed. It had been built using a technique that meant unless particularly experienced demolition experts were called in to bring down the building in a properly controlled manner, all kinds of metal objects of considerable weight could be shot into the homes, gardens and business premises of the neighbours. While this sounds rather melodramatic, architect Terry Ward made it abundantly clear that there was a real and present danger. In the end, so confident were the RFU in its demolition team that guests were invited to sit in the new North Stand to watch the old South Stand levelled, with covers put over half the pitch to protect it from debris. The demolition took place on Sunday, 10 July 2005, and while there were guests watching, a wider plan for festivities to mark the disappearance of the structure were cancelled in the wake of the 7 July terror attacks in the centre of London.

Ward remembers: 'The old South Stand was constructed using post-tensioned, pre-stressed, in-situ concrete. The concrete had been made off-site with steel reinforcement already inside and they put tension on the steel on-site. They pulled the steel, which increased the camber to allow it to take more weight. They locked them in, but that meant when it came to knocking it down, you could have steel bolts flying as if from a cannon because they were under severe tension. We used a very experienced demolition company and they were fully aware of the problems, and they were very good. It did exactly what they said the stand would do when they blew it up – it imploded. Nothing flew out of the stadium!

'There was a sigh of relief when it went well. The stand had been opened by Hector Munro and it replaced the cinder hill that they cemented over to create a terrace. The old stand we demolished in 2007 wasn't a rugby stand, and there were two at racecourses in England and I saw another in Abu Dhabi. Next to the stand were these vertically stacked Portakabins that served as hospitality areas. Those had to go when the stand went.'

When the button to detonate the 60 kilograms of dynamite packed into the 5,000 tonnes of old South Stand was pushed, after a warning flare had been launched to signal the imminent explosion, it took three or four seconds for it to actually happen. The *Richmond and Twickenham Times* spoke to Holly Bennett, the explosives engineer from Controlled Demolition, the group given the task of reducing the stand to rubble without impacting on the surrounding homes. The paper reported:

> Residents from 117 homes around the stand will be evacuated while the operation takes place and most will watch the explosion while enjoying hospitality in the stadium. Planning for the operation took three months and the 15-week project began on June 27 when the 14-strong demolition team removed asbestos from the stand and stripped it of fixtures and fittings such as the seats. Holly Bennett, explosives engineer for the Controlled Demolition group, explained how it all works. 'We do a little pre-weakening to the stand. Take out very small sections of the structure and then put in small pieces of explosives.' The engineers spread the 60kg of dynamite across 1,500 individual charges to demolish the stadium. Holly said: 'We put timings in different sections inside the stand which is how we determine which way the building falls. It will look like it is going to come practically straight down but it is going to be tilting back very slightly away from the pitch so the roof doesn't fall onto the pitch. Everyone thinks it is going to be a massive explosion. But it is the safest form of demolition; because the explosives are inside the concrete the explosion is

muffled. There will be some dust but not as much as people think there is going to be. In a way it is quite sad, I have been a big rugby union fan all my life, my dad can't believe that I am knocking down Twickenham, but it is good and making way for new things.[2]

Holly's confidence was well placed and the dust cloud that erupted as the stand fell neatly like a pack of cards barely reached the halfway line. 'It was really quiet and there was just a lot of smoke,' said Victoria Wiseman, a Chudleigh Road resident who lived just 100 metres from the stadium and was invited in to watch. 'We saw the top bit fall into the bottom half, then there was a lot of dust and then it was really quiet. It was a nice atmosphere. When we were still sitting there the street cleaners were out. There was dust on cars but we were told to expect it.'

Road sweepers were on standby to deal with any mess, while the debris of the smashed stand was turned into rubble to be recycled as a base for the new structure. The building of the South Stand created considerable debate locally and within local government, with the then Mayor of London, Ken Livingstone, making it clear that the scheme had to come up with traffic-management ideas and public-transport proposals. Given a lack of interest from anyone to actually fund an extension to any of the potential Underground links, the only possible improvement was going to involve Twickenham station, which had been opened in 1950 and

---

2 *Richmond and Twickenham Times.*

was in desperate need of regeneration. Fans getting off the train at Twickenham have two possible exits manned by numerous station staff, although the pace is hardly more than a shuffle during peak periods as the station just wasn't designed for the number of people who use it on match days.

While the transport issues were top of the agenda, even the harshest critics of the development could see the introduction of a four-star hotel, leisure club and arts facilities for use by the community would have plus points. It wasn't all going to be bad news for the local economy and residents. The fact that England became Rugby World Cup winners in 2003 boosted the profile of the game and made Twickenham a natural focal point for the sport in the country. With twenty-two houses to be flattened to make way for the new stand and an initial idea to have an extra floor to boost hotel-room numbers to 200, residents facing the proposed development expressed their anger at having hotel guests looking out of their bedroom windows down into theirs!

Richmond Council's planning committee approved the new South Stand development at a meeting in December 2003. The *Richmond and Twickenham Times* reported:

> The decision followed a marathon four and a half hour meeting in which councillors weighed up the concerns of the stand's immediate neighbours with the potential benefits for the whole borough. The current stand and 14 Victorian houses will be demolished, to be replaced with a new stand, boosting the stadium's capacity by 7,500 to 82,000. There will also

be a new 200-bedroom hotel, health and leisure club, conference and exhibition centre, basement parking, new ticket sales facilities, and a new shop and offices for the RFU in the £70m project. Two blocks of flats will also be built. The announcement has largely been welcomed by community leaders who say it will bring new jobs and major economic spin-offs. The decision is subject to approval from the Government Office for London and the Mayor of London.[3]

Twickenham Councillor David Porter summed up the dilemma faced by the planning committee, saying: 'It is difficult with a case like this because the benefits of the scheme are very wide and global, and will be broadly beneficial for Twickenham. But this comes at a cost to a small number of residents.' The *Richmond and Twickenham Times*, which has charted the unfolding story of the stadium through its pages, reflected the concerns of the residents and quoted Robert Irvine, chairman of the Whitton Road residents' association, who said: 'There will be a massive loss of privacy; guests from the hotel will be able to look into our homes.' He explained they knew when they moved in they were living opposite a rugby ground, but did not realise it would become 'Blackpool Illuminations with a hotel'. He added that because of its sheer size it would be 'like living opposite a skyscraper'.

In the end the new South Stand did not have an underground car park and the capacity of the hotel was reduced to 156 rooms – something the RFU would regret once the

---

3 *Richmond and Twickenham Times.*

facility became a popular convention and conference destination. Stadium architect Ward said, 'The new South Stand was the last chance for the RFU to diversify and to maximise whatever they could. You had to be doing your homework harder when you were now dealing with a professional management at the RFU but they also did their preparation work. I did an outline for Francis Baron, the chief executive, and it was incorporated in their forward plan and the idea was to get planning permission for as much as we thought we could get away with, and that included a 200-room hotel with underground car parking, which we got permission for in 2003. It was unusual because it was the type of permission you would get in a city centre, not suburbia, and Richmond were very good from that point of view.

'The RFU then spent most of 2004 finding out what they could afford to build and that was the difference with the professional management. The feasibility at that time suggested that if the hotel could meet an occupancy of 61 to 62 per cent it would be fine and it is actually running at 70 per cent. The South Stand cost between £130m and £140m and it was a big risk because the RFU were the developers and there were a lot of negotiations between Twickenham Experience and Marriott. I was lucky enough to go out with Paul Vaughan, the RFU business operations director, to meet J.W. Marriott, the hotel company founder, who told us stories about his university days. He went on tour to New Zealand and Australia and while he didn't play he enjoyed the experience. He had remarkable enthusiasm for the Twickenham project.'

The South Stand bowl, with a seating capacity of 20,000,

was opened in 2006 by Tessa Jowell MP in time for the November international with New Zealand. The Rugby Store, the main retail outlet at the stadium, occupies over 7,000 square feet in the new complex, with the Marriott Hotel opening its doors for business in 2009. The following year, the RFU staff moved from their offices opposite the East Stand into the newly developed Rugby House, based in the South Stand.

The completion of the South Stand complex signalled the end of the Ward/Hallett double act at Twickenham. Their job had been done – the stadium was the bowl that had always been envisaged. It had taken far longer than either man expected and not everything they had come up with made it from drawing board to actuality. 'Tony and I always said we would have a hotel and swimming pool as part of the stadium development and we talked long and hard about having a Hilton Hotel in the west car park. We have ended up with a hotel in the South Stand with a 25-metre pool in the Virgin Active health club, and so we did get there in the end!'

Ward never factored in music concerts when he designed Twickenham but the most famous rugby venue in the world has more than acceptable acoustics, as can be registered on match days when 'Swing Low, Sweet Chariot' erupts from the 82,000. 'The stadium was never designed for concerts and I cannot take any credit for the good sound that it generates. I was interested in ensuring it was a good atmosphere for rugby as I am a debenture holder in the West Stand in the middle tier, just off centre behind the commentators. Stadia are only ever good when they are full and when I have seen aerial pictures of the completed bowl at Twickenham, it reminds me a bit of the Coliseum with the repetitive structure, and it is a gladiatorial arena.

'Around three sides of the ground the staircases are on a double spiral, which I am quite proud about. That is unusual and we did it to have a lot of staircase capacity to cope with 82,000, and they were designed so that a set of staircases gave access to the middle tier, and rising above that spiral is another set for the upper tier. There are links in case people get out onto the wrong level. We also put escalators in, making it the first stadium to have escalators in that kind of number.'

Building the new-look Twickenham wasn't totally dominated by the bigger picture, and Hallett and Ward were always looking for something different to make the development more than just a successful concrete and steel addition to the local skyline.

For many years there have been rumours of a 'Project X' in the RFU halls of power at Twickenham. What is not generally known is that there were two other Projects – Y and Z – although the final one never got off the planning board. It was drawn up by Hallett, who oversaw the redevelopment of the stadium before assuming – for around three years – the role of secretary after Dudley Wood. It would be a turbulent time in the life of the Union, marked by internal warfare in an organisation desperately trying to come to terms with a game that had turned professional in 1995. Although Hallett left the secretary's post in 1998, his legacy remains in the form of the 'new' Twickenham and Projects X and Y.

With RFU treasurer Peter Bromage working his wonders

with NatWest bank, Hallett was given the green light on the various budgets needed to build the North, East and West Stands, and it was within those costs for the stadium that room was found for three pet projects. The first to come to life was Project Y, which involved the installation of four sculptures on the Rowland Hill Gates produced by Gerald Laing, who would later also cast in bronze the line-out statue which stands in the South Stand piazza. His son Farquhar was incredibly persistent in contacting Hallett, who eventually agreed to meet him. The result was the commissioning, for around £250,000, of four statues depicting 'Kicker', 'Winger', 'Scrum Half' and 'Forward'. Hallett said: 'I had said it was important to break up the concrete and put a bit of culture in the place and Gerald Laing's son pursued me all over the country, and he was so persuasive that I ended up having lunch with him in the Chelsea Arts Club. As a result, we slipped the statues in – on a costed basis without exactly saying what it was – as Project Y.'

Having successfully completed Project Y and avoided any unwanted queries from fellow committee members, Hallett moved on to the two remaining projects and he found considerable support for 'X' – the building of a cellar to house the wine that secretary Dudley Wood knew was accumulating from England's long-standing opponents (who were all wine-producing countries: France, New Zealand, South Africa and Australia). Hallett explained: 'In those days there was an air of trust that may not be so evident now. I wouldn't agree that it was Dudley's original idea for Project X, and all three projects were my suggestions – as I remember it! Project X was to be a wine cellar featuring the shields of the Five Nations but it was becoming clear we would shortly need to add Italy who were going to make it a Six Nations Championship. The shields were cast in materials from each of those six nations. We put in a refectory table and got in touch with Paul Morgan, who specialised in designing wine cellars. He was also the father of Olly Morgan, the England full-back who played at Gloucester. Paul came up to London and showed us how he would design the cellar with brick and featuring bins for all the wine the RFU had been given. It cost around £80,000 to put in and looking back it was a snip of a price.'

As Hallett had a good working relationship with Terry Ward, the stadium architect, it was natural to take his plan for Project X to him so that it could be successfully included in the drawings for the West Stand. To ensure no one actually realised it was a cellar, it was built on the second floor – close to the large Spirit of Rugby dining area. To give it even more of a mysterious air, fire doors were put as a layer in front of the actual panel doors that open into the magnificent dining area. Ward also remembers the discussion about trying to break up the concrete look of the new stadium and has his own view on who actually came up with Project X (it seems incredible that, with an increasingly large number in the 'know', so few within the Union actually know the genesis of their special wine cellar). Ward said: 'I got some feedback from the RFU and one of the questions they asked after the three stands had been erected was, were we going to dress the stadium like Wimbledon with creepers growing up the walls! I wanted to put sculptures around the stadium and Dudley wrote back and said that his idea was to have a wine cellar because England played against all the best wine-producing countries in the world, and if there was a cellar in the West Stand the RFU would get gifts from all of those countries.

'We designed a wine cellar on Level Two but then Tony Hallett got hold of the idea. We would have built a concrete floor and racked it out and temperature-controlled it. Suddenly, we had a presentation by a company at the East India Club and they had turned it into something that looked like it was from the time of *The Three Musketeers*. It has a terracotta floor, French oak barrels and a pair of doors that look like they came off a thirteenth-century cathedral. They are behind a pair of grey-painted doors with fire warnings on them, which means you don't notice anything until you open them and there are the cathedral doors with strap hinges. It does knock you out. When it was first opened it was designed for fifteen people to sit down and I had reports of more than forty in the place, and we had to put extra air conditioning in because the heat that was being generated was starting to affect all the wine in there. It has hosted John Major and [Irish Deputy PM] Dick Spring, who held private talks, along with other high-profile visitors. It is now used by sponsors and, having cost £98,000 to fit out, in the first year it was sponsored and brought in nearly £70,000 in the late 1990s, and so it's paid for itself many times over.'

Wood's hope that England's opponents would be generous with their gifts of wine proved correct and a considerable stock of fine bottles were collected with an estimated worth of £250,000. The wine became a prized asset and when the Union was in dire financial straits in 1998, Francis Baron, the Union's newly appointed (and first) chief executive, was amazed to find he was sitting on a wine windfall. 'When I looked at the balance sheet, I saw that there was an item of £250,000 which was just wine,' recalled Baron. 'That is a lot for an organisation like the RFU who, at that time, were trying to deal with substantial debts. I sold it all to the hospitality people Payne and Gunter for £250,000 because I took the view it was inappropriate to have so much money in wine. I don't think anyone knew we had that much wine in the cellar. Tony [Hallett] built the wonderful cellar and called it Project X because, I assume, he didn't want anyone to know about it. It is now part of the hospitality facilities of the stadium which can be rented out on match days and it makes good money because it is unique. Tony is a great guy and the cellar has been very well used over the years.'

Project Z was the one that fell by the wayside, as Hallett confessed: 'Project Z was a walk-in humidor and that never came to pass because of the change in attitudes to smoking, and it was never pursued. These projects were on the spreadsheet with all the costings and went before the finance committee with no one actually asking what X, Y and Z meant! It was extraordinary and so we paid for £250,000 of statues. This was all happening before the West Stand was actually built.'

Hallett is heavily involved in a new project to develop the ground where his beloved Richmond play their rugby – ironically, one of the most obvious alternative options when the RFU chose to base themselves on the other bank of the Thames in Twickenham in 1907. He is proud of the stadium he helped create and paid tribute to another key man in the upgrading of the home of English rugby. 'Peter Bromage deserves a lot of credit for the development of Twickenham, as the treasurer after Sandy Sanders, and he used to say to me, "You build it, Hallett, and I will pay for it." He spent considerable time in the main NatWest office in the City arranging the loan and repayment schedule and it was a fascinating time. What also drove us in what we were doing was seeing how Scotland were dealing with the rebuilding of Murrayfield. They issued debentures over fifteen years, while ours were five-, seven- or ten-year renewals. I think the West Stand is my favourite as the ultimate creation but to finish the bowl was fantastic. I am immensely proud of the stadium and one thing I always wanted to do was break up the concrete and that's why we went for the statues. However, my idea was to put a Hilton Hotel in the west car park but that wasn't popular! '

In the view of Wood, the stadium development has been a success, although he does accept the sheer size of Twickenham has not pleased everyone. 'There are some things I regret: firstly that spectators are a long way from the pitch if they are at the top of the stands. But it can't be helped if you are going to get 82,000 people in for an international. You don't get the intimate feel that used to be a feature of the old stadium, although they are working hard to ensure the atmosphere is good. I went in 2013 for an international match and walked up to the stadium from the station and really needed the loo. I asked one of the stewards on the gate as I went in, "Where is the nearest gents' toilet," and she asked, "Have you ever been here before?" and had to admit that I had – before she was born!'

When the Welsh Rugby Union built the Millennium Stadium on the footprint of the old Arms Park, right in the heart of Cardiff, they added a roof to make it unique among major rugby stadia. Twickenham is open to the elements and there were only cursory discussions about putting a retractable roof on the stadium, as Wood revealed: 'We did discuss a roof, but it was considered too expensive. It was never a serious possibility at Twickenham.'

Chapter Three

Harlequins – the multi-coloured first tenants

In 1909, Harlequins signed a lease with the Rugby Football Union to use the new national stadium in Twickenham, and the first club match took place that year. In those early days, only one or two internationals were played during the season, and it wasn't long before the RFU ground became the recognised headquarters of the Harlequins Football Club. They would continue to call it home until, in 1963, the Quins acquired an athletics ground with fourteen acres just across the A316 from Twickenham, which became the Harlequins training pitch. The RFU's choice of Twickenham had been confusing for Harlequins members as well as the rest of the game. In his book *Immortal Harlequin* Ian Cooper states:

> A twenty-one-year lease could have been secured [by the RFU] on Richmond with provision of a new stand costing £3,000. Of the ten acres [the RFU bought], eight were to be used for a football ground, the remaining two to be sold for building purposes. Following the purchase of the ground, £1,606.9s 4d had been spent in the first year and a further £8,000 in 1908, largely on drainage, road improvements, entrances, mounds and terraces. On 27 November 1908 the RFU received the formal letter on behalf of the Harlequins about sharing the new ground at Twickenham.

It was Adrian Stoop, one of the most famous of all Harlequins, who signed an agreement in 1909 on behalf of the club as head lessee of the new ground for the 'princely sum' of a hundred guineas per season. Stoop immediately requested a further three years on top of the two that had been initially agreed and this was granted. In typical Quins style, they set about trying to make the ground their own by arranging for shandy and lemons to be made available for refreshment of the crowd on match days. The *Thames Valley Times* reported that around 3,500 fans turned up for the very first match to be played at Twickenham, which saw Harlequins defeat Richmond – the occasion did not include any formal opening of the stadium. In 1959, to mark fifty years of the ground's first match, a combined side made

up of players from England and Wales beat a team repre-
senting Ireland and Scotland 26–17.

Discussion during and after that first match revolved
around two issues; firstly the length of the grass, which
many felt was too long for rugby union, and secondly the
distance that had to be travelled on foot from Twickenham
station to reach the stadium. The general acceptance of
English rugby's new home was summed up by the *Thames
Valley Times*, whose correspondent noted: 'Whether it was
wanted or not is not a question to go into here. It has been
established and it is for the Rugby Union itself to make it
pay without – and this is a very important point – doing any
injury to any of the grounds of the metropolitan clubs who,
be it remembered, have largely helped in the accumulation
of the funds which have made the establishment of the new
ground possible.' Although it had many detractors, a trip to
the ground did provide Harlequins with some benefits, with
club rules allowing any male member to invite two ladies
free of charge as spectators for matches at Twickenham.

Harlequins had full use of the Twickenham pitch until
the internationals were played, with the pitch merely rolled
flat after each game, which contributed to the poor state
of the surface during bad weather periods. The use of a
roller was only stopped when Harold Clark became clerk of
works in 1964 and decreed that the only place for a roller at
Twickenham was rusting in a shed. With their raft of famous
players, Harlequins were worthy tenants of the home of
English rugby, and with their multi-coloured jerseys they
certainly stood out from the crowd. It was tradition at the
stadium that the ground staff would hand-paint the names

of the two teams playing at Twickenham that day, with the signs being hung outside the respective changing rooms. This meant using all the colours in the Harlequins kit to make up their name and then, for example, dark blue for London Scottish. Not surprisingly, those team-name plates became collector's items, hence the need for a sign-writing room under the North Stand.

Colin Herridge was secretary of Harlequins from 1981 to 1994, was on the RFU Committee from 1986 to 1997, and acted as media liaison officer for the England team under manager Jack Rowell. Herridge spent many years sitting in the Twickenham committee box watching his team play in front of ever-diminishing spectator numbers. He said, 'As a club, we had the right to play at least thirteen games a season at Twickenham Stadium for a nominal hundred guineas. Then more England games were arranged for the autumn period along with other fixtures and we found that we had less and less opportunities to use the stadium. At the same time we were developing the Stoop, putting together plans for a new stand and creating our own stadium. By the time we got to the early 1990s we only played two or three games at Twickenham and as secretary of the club I felt we were two different clubs – one played at Twickenham and the other at the Stoop. The two never met because those who took part in a first-team fixture drank in a bar the RFU made available to us in the old West Stand while the rest of the Harlequins teams were meeting at the Stoop.

'We told the RFU at the start of the 1990s that we were going to play at the Stoop, which did change the nature of our season. Using Twickenham Stadium meant playing our home games before Christmas – before the internationals – and then our away games in the second half of the season. By playing at Twickenham during the first half of the season, the pitch was in pretty good shape compared to later in the year. We could get good clubs, including the leading Welsh teams, because we were at Twickenham and we attracted crowds of more than 10,000. The problems came when we played Gloucester on a county championship day, which meant the majority of their players were with Gloucestershire and we had eight with Middlesex. As a result, there would be barely 200 fans at Twickenham – it was morbid.'

Harlequins now play in front of sell-out 14,300 crowds at the Twickenham Stoop – as it has been renamed – although they do hire the national stadium once a year for their Big Game matches. These attract near sell-out attendances and maintain a link with the stadium that stretches back to that first match in 1909. 'As far as I know, the original agreement signed by Adrian Stoop has never been torn up and we must still have the right for a hundred guineas to play thirteen matches on the Twickenham Stadium pitch!' added Herridge, who could save the club a large rental charge if he chose to implement the agreement!

Chapter Four

Travelling to Twickenham Stadium – the recurring nightmare

When the Prince of Wales opened the new RFU offices at Twickenham in 1977 he arrived and departed – waving to the staff – in a helicopter. Clearly, the future king had been well briefed about the problems of travelling to the home of English rugby by car from central London. From the very moment the site was chosen for the new national stadium in 1907, considerable disquiet was expressed due to the distance from Piccadilly Circus and the fact that the RFU had decided to build a ground in a country setting. Patently, the Union were operating along the lines of, 'If you build it they will come,' and despite the difficulties associated with getting to Twickenham from all corners of the realm, they can claim to have been right.

What has constantly hampered the development of the stadium is a total lack of communication and agreement between the various transport authorities and the RFU over moving large numbers of rugby fans to TW2. The London and South West Railway initially refused to build a new stop at Whitton, while Twickenham Urban Council didn't want an Underground link from Richmond and the first bus service from central London to Twickenham station didn't arrive until 1924. This followed a demand a year earlier from local police and residents for proper transport links. Frustration at a lack of help led to the RFU reportedly seeking a new site for the home of English rugby, but given the expense involved, they decided to stay.

Twickenham's choice as English rugby's home coincided with the arrival of the motor car as a means of popular transport in Britain. However, the area around the stadium was made up of country roads more used to the horse and cart, and certainly not buses or cars. This was due, in part, to the lack of a crossing over the Thames to link the area with the centre of the capital, and it wasn't until 1932 that Twickenham Bridge was built on the Great Chertsey Road, which meant drivers could avoid having to travel through Richmond and across the bridge in the town to reach the stadium. The Great Chertsey Road artery would not be designated a class-one motor route until 1937 – fully thirty years after the RFU chose Twickenham as its home. When the stadium was first built, the RFU spent £20,000 – a considerable sum in those days – on roads and entrances to ensure there was adequate access for the first match staged at the new ground, between Harlequins and Richmond in 1909. Quins won 14–10 and Adrian Stoop played for the winners. The initial capacity was 30,000, with parking for 200 vehicles that were left by their owners all over the allocated area. The west car park was flooded by the River Crane in 1927 and again the following year, which didn't really paint the stadium in a very favourable light for those early car owners.

For those without access to a car, the only way to get to Twickenham if you didn't live locally was the overground railway which started from Waterloo. The *Thames Valley Times* greeted the first club game by recording that 'the hyper-critical will doubtless find some points to grumble about . . . one objection to the ground has been the distance from the station. One scribe said it took him 12 minutes to do the walk. All we can say is that he would stand a poor chance in the Marathon.' The *Richmond and Twickenham Times* said that opinions on the ground were divided and noted the walk from the station 'may be a little uncomfortable on wet days'. The first international against Wales kicked off fifteen minutes late due to congestion as fans tried to get into the new home of English rugby. A general election was taking place, leading some to speculate that fans were delayed because they had been voting. One of the England players was late turning up because the milk train from Cornwall had been delayed and one consequence was the absence of time to take the usual team photographs.

In an attempt to improve the situation, adverts appeared around London urging fans to travel to the game by tram from Hammersmith or Shepherd's Bush using the London United Tramway Company. They claimed it was an eight-minute walk to the stadium once you alighted. In 1925, the local police had to enlist the help of European royalty to ensure that fans arriving in motor vehicles were able to get to the ground in time to see the infamous match with New Zealand that saw Kiwi Cyril Brownlie sent off in a game watched by the Prince of Wales and Prime Minister Stanley Baldwin. The narrow country roads around the stadium were clogged with hundreds of cars, which created long lines of stationary traffic – much like the scene on the A316 today before kick-off. There was a real danger of fans not getting to the ground on time and only the quick thinking of the local police provided an answer. Faced with a long line of cars, the officers sought help from an ex-king, Manuel II of Portugal, who owned the large Fulwell Park estate in the local area, and he agreed to a request to let the cars divert across his land to get to the stadium. Manuel's estate has been swallowed up by suburban housing but one unique part of his life in the area remains in the form of the four-tonne safe that used to house the royal jewels, which is now to be found in a Hampton church – minus the loot.

In his expertly researched book, *Twickenham: The History of the Cathedral of Rugby,* Ed Harris recalls the comments of a local estate agent early in the life of Twickenham Stadium who tried to entice would-be buyers to the area as 'no noisy tramcar or motor omnibus to make both the day and night hideous and the lives of your wives and children unsafe, but absolute country quiet and seclusion within 29 minutes of London's centre'. That estate agent could not have summed up better the reasons why Twickenham was a problem for fans to reach and such a controversial choice by the RFU.

Despite the arrival of Whitton station, an upgraded Twickenham station, the widening of the A316 and the introduction of free buses to transport fans from Richmond and Hounslow to the ground, nothing has been done to drastically improve the situation for travelling fans since the 1930s. The long lines of fans queuing after a match to get onto the platforms at Twickenham station show incredible patience given it is a scene that should not be witnessed in these times of modern transport solutions to mass travel. However, Twickenham station is too small, the roads are too small and the area around the stadium is too small for 82,000 fans. The introduction of post-match entertainment and the increase in the number of bars helps stagger the departure of staggering fans, and this is one way the stadium tries to lessen the impact on the public transport system and the local area.

The number of car parks have, over the years, been increased with the RFU purchasing land at Rosebine Avenue, which has now taken over as one of the main parking options following the decision to radically change the nature of the stadium's west car park. This used to be *the* spot to get before a match but the grass area that used to become home to some of the most fabulous car-boot feasts before a game (and would allow French fans to wander between vehicles loudly requesting and receiving food and drink from home fans) is now very different. Part of the car park is used by the South Stand hotel for guest parking during the week and no longer allows open-plan picnicking. The rest of the car park is dominated by a large-screen TV, retail and food-outlet vans, a double-decker marquee with public bar and karaoke below and sponsors area above, the O2 tent that offers the team sponsor a chance to look after its guests, and row upon row of mobile toilets.

The Cardinal Vaughan car park has now assumed the role of the first-choice picnic option if you are lucky enough to get a ticket for that area, which is linked to the stadium by a small bridge. The school rugby pitches on which the cars are parked look particularly lush because they have the turf that was removed from the Twickenham pitch when the new Desso surface was installed. The north car park is gravelled instead of the grass surface that allowed fans to put out rugs behind their cars and fold-up chairs, as this becomes the main car park for the stadium during the working week. There are also lines of Portakabins where on-site building workers congregate for their orders, and others are designated for the temporary catering staff who start arriving, fresh-faced, hours before they have to deliver thousands of meals to hospitality clients. The north car park also serves as a parking area for the host of mobile catering vehicles when not required on match days. The small east car park no longer exists, a blow to the press corps who used to enjoy their own small area of picnic heaven just behind the East Stand where they have always operated. The arrival of Tesco close to the stadium not only gave the Twickenham staff an easy way to do their shopping, it also provided a new, large car-parking area, and the store closes early on match days so that it can be transformed into an official area for cars. It is the only Tesco store anywhere in the supermarket world that does not stay open on Saturday afternoons.

Today, the control of traffic revolves around a joint effort by safety stewards employed by the RFU – more than a thousand are on duty on match days – and the local police. The sheer volume of fans moving from Twickenham station and then along Whitton Road to the large roundabout on the A316, means that all traffic has to be halted close to kick-off time as the number of supporters fills the width of the road. Police on horseback control the flow of the fans across one of the main roads into London with incredible good humour and understanding. Due to the volume of pedestrians and traffic around the stadium, a number of roads are typically closed for around one-and-a-half to two hours before the start of an event, and then again at the end of the event for about a couple of hours. When large crowds are expected on an event day – over 25,000 is the criteria – the 'Twickenham Event Zone' is introduced, also known as Community Parking Zone R. This is a one-day community parking zone around the stadium. Where the crowd is more than 30,000, the full CPZ is usually implemented, covering a large number of roads in the area. Some residents in these prime locations offer car-parking places on their forecourts for £20 a vehicle. Others with much larger frontages receive considerably more for allowing burger vans and memorabilia outlets to park up and make the most of tens of thousands walking past. Whitton Road takes on the appearance of a bazaar, and everything from doughnuts, Cornish pasties and South African braai food to Ref Link – the radio receiver that allows you to hear the match referee during the game – can be purchased from front gardens.

Of course, with more than 4,000 parking places on offer and hundreds more vehicles parked wherever fans can find a place outside the permit exclusion zone, Twickenham, Whitton, Richmond, Teddington, Hounslow and Brentford become almost no-go areas on match days unless you're heading for the stadium. But, as residents and fans will tell you, that is the norm for Twickenham's transport system and – barring a miracle – it always will be.

A mass-transport solution would have been one of the answers to all of the car problems. Many have tried but all have failed to come up with a way of linking Twickenham Stadium to the London Underground tube network. It would help solve some of the most difficult transport headaches that have bedevilled the stadium ever since Cail and Williams decided Twickenham was the best choice for the home of English rugby. With the District line stopping at Richmond and the Piccadilly line travelling to the north of the stadium, through Osterley and Hounslow, tapping into these transport arteries has been a recurring desire that remains frustratingly out of reach. Dudley Wood, the former secretary, still harbours the hope that one day the District line map will include a station in the Twickenham west car park where, in the 1980s, he envisaged a park-and-ride car park for commuters, who battle their way towards London on the M3 before it becomes the A316 and passes close to the stadium.

'I went ten rounds with London Underground about putting a new station in the west car park. That failed but I still believe it could be a major asset. I offered ground for a station, realising that traffic came up and still comes up the

M3 and A316 and comes to a grinding halt very near to the stadium. My attitude was, here were we with car parks empty from Monday to Friday and money could be made from the situation and it would also be a major asset on match days. My idea was that the tube trains would go along the railway lines from Richmond to Twickenham and then head underground through a tunnel to the west car park. They came back and said British Rail don't want to have underground trains on their lines to Twickenham and, secondly, "We don't have any money." I believe that Boris Johnson, the Mayor of London, should be brought into the discussions because he gets things done. Access to Twickenham Stadium on match days remains the biggest problem. There was talk of putting in a new line through to Heathrow from London Transport and it is a missed opportunity. I really don't know how people manage to get to the stadium because the M25 can be a real problem.'

The pressure to solve the transport headaches of the stadium also exercised Terry Ward, the architect who was masterminding Twickenham's redevelopment into an 82,000-seat arena that would only increase the need to get people to and from events quickly. Having joined the company that built the Channel Tunnel, while dealing with the new stand construction, Ward was in a unique position to bounce ideas off experts in taking mass transport underground. Ward chose to look at the Piccadilly line option rather than the District line at Richmond as the bridge over the Thames that carries trains had restricted capacity. What was needed was a tunnel from Osterley station that made use of the large area covered by the Mogden sewage works to the north of Twickenham Stadium, to minimise the impact on residential areas. Ward, like Wood, remains a keen supporter of an Underground link despite the obvious stumbling block: Who is going to pay for it?

Ward said, 'We had wonderful plans for a cut-and-cover tunnel from Osterley station to Twickenham Stadium on the Piccadilly line and have a station in the north car park. You would have excavated the tunnel and then covered it, which is a cheaper way of providing a tunnel. The trouble with the District line is the bridge over the Thames and they have serious problems with timetabling. Coming from the north is much easier and we did look at that in the 1990s during Tony Hallett's most visionary period. Extending the Piccadilly line would have been fantastic but we didn't get any government support for the idea. Osterley was the shortest distance to the rugby ground and the majority of the line would have gone through Mogden sewage works, and that wouldn't have been too much of a problem in terms of residential homes. We were then part of Mott MacDonald, who designed the Channel Tunnel, and we had contacts and put the idea forward – but it fell on deaf ears. It was capable of being done and it is still possible. We also made representations to the Department for Culture, Media and Sport about supporting the bid to host the Olympics. We had reconfigured the stadium to provide an athletics track and would put it back to a rugby stadium after the Games. If we had [been accepted] we would have got the support for the transport ideas.'

Gaining support from the government for such an expensive undertaking was, and remains, absolutely vital and Francis Baron, during his time as RFU chief executive, raised the issue of improving transport links with government departments, and the answer was always the same. 'Politicians are great at saying it's a good idea and then they add that "the Treasury is not going to allow us to do it yet".' Discussions with Chancellor Gordon Brown failed to break the deadlock. He continued, 'It is difficult to get a decision out of a body like Transport for London and we had discussions with Boris Johnson when he was elected London Mayor, and all the schemes that would have made a difference needed too many people to agree and the costs were really very serious. You are talking a billion pounds to extend the Piccadilly line. I had a massive file in my office at Twickenham with plans and correspondence but nothing really came of anything and it's very hard to see how the position is going to change. The brand is Twickenham and in my time there was never any thought of being anywhere else and with the new stands, you are there for good, which means managing the situation with traffic and transport. Wembley, Lord's and Wimbledon have their own transport problems because of history – they are in places where modern-day transport issues are very difficult.'

The 2015 Rugby World Cup provided another major sporting event to concentrate minds on the Underground and rail issues of Twickenham Stadium. What happened only served to confirm all that Wood, Ward and Baron had highlighted about the problems of pulling together all the groups needed to ensure fundamental change to the rail transport system for Twickenham can be implemented. In the run-up to the World Cup, a battle between residents and Richmond Council ended in May 2013 with the Court of Appeal dismissing an appeal to overturn the planning decision about Twickenham station's redevelopment made two years earlier. Although the council won their case, the legal wrangle put in doubt whether the redevelopment would be ready in time for the World Cup. Leader of the council Lord True said: 'Twickenham station is a disgrace and, while this whole process has resulted in massive delays to the developers' schedule, I now hope that they can make enough progress to be able to deliver a twenty-first-century station in time for the Rugby World Cup in 2015 when the eyes of the world will be on our town.' However, Tim Shoveller, managing director of the Network Rail and South West Trains Alliance, confirmed that 'Because of the delay caused by the legal challenge, it will no longer be possible to deliver all the elements of this regeneration project in time for the 2015 Rugby World Cup. We are drawing up an alternative programme which will focus on delivering an improved temporary station and public area by 2015 while delivering elements of the wider development after the Rugby World Cup. Network Rail has agreed with the Mayor of London and London Borough of Richmond a package of platform enhancements at Twickenham on top of the platform extensions that are currently being built. These will deliver significant improvements for passengers and help ease congestion at the station.'[4]

---

4   May 2013, Yourlocal Guardian.co.uk

Chapter Five

Harold and John Clark create a family dynasty before it all goes Desso

When Twickenham was chosen to become the home of English rugby, one of the first tasks was to work out exactly where the pitch would be created in the former orchards. This was achieved with the rather rudimentary use of four chairs to act as corners and, once the right position had been established, everything else could take shape around it. The main problem with the area was the clay soil that would be a constant headache for those charged with the turf's upkeep; even today, after the installation of a £1.25m state-of-the-art Desso pitch in 2012, the battle against the elements and the local conditions remains as intense as ever.

The main worry in 1907 was the local river that threatened to flood the new pitch. It was decided to raise the pitch above the local land, which meant that for many decades the players went up a short set of steps onto the Twickenham pitch. The cost of draining and turfing the area more than a century ago was £1,012 6s 11d. The pitch level was created with the help of Charles Crane, then president of the RFU, who arranged for spoil from the Metropolitan line – which was in the process of being built – to be dumped on the site. This elevated the pitch by 2 feet, and current head groundsman Keith Kent reports the clay soil from those far-off days is still providing the bed on which all subsequent pitches have been laid. Over the years, those charged with the upkeep of the most famous ground in world rugby have been forced to devise new techniques to combat the heavy soil and the overuse of the pitch, particularly when Harlequins were still playing the majority of their club fixtures at HQ.

'Twickenham in the early days, and for quite a long time afterwards, was an ordinary field on which cattle, sheep or horses grazed when it was not required for matches,' Philip Warner wrote in his history of the Harlequins. The first groundsman is believed to have been George A. Street, who laid out the pitch, but Charles Hale is widely acknowledged as being the first to be considered the 'groundsman'. The Hale family would have a major influence on the pitch in the period leading up to the 1960s when Harold Clark arrived and assumed the role, appropriately, of Twickenham's first clerk of works. His arrival revolutionised the running of the stadium and brought to an end what can only be described as a slipshod regime that RFU officials appeared to completely ignore. It would be fair to assume that the Union top brass were happy to let the status quo continue on the basis that matches were successfully staged on what was generally accepted to be a mud bath. When the mud wasn't in evidence, the grass was allowed to grow long in a bid to protect the surface – particularly from frost.

Harlequins played their home matches on it, and there were also the Home Internationals along with various other fixtures. Each one added to the problems, with the surface being churned up and the pitch merely rolled to get it back into playable condition. This only served to compact an already substandard surface and, although the RFU did seek professional help in the years preceding Clark's arrival, no answer had been found to the drainage problems. Spiking to various depths was tried and numerous experts cast their educated eyes over the turf, but only Clark took the action that was needed to really address the problem – he ploughed Twickenham up! It was something he would repeat every four years in May and then use a reported 'half a ton of seed' – rye grass was his chosen variety – to create a new surface that would be ready for the next season. He then instigated what would become his 'invention' – a sand-slitting technique which made Twickenham the best-drained ground in the world. 'Unfortunately, I never made a penny out of this invention,' he later lamented. Harold Clark was in charge of Twickenham from St Valentine's Day 1964 until 3 April 1982 and would be replaced, after an interview process, by his son John, who held the position for a further twenty-six years. Both Clarks would see fundamental changes to the stadium during their careers at Twickenham but it was Harold who faced the most serious problems.

When Harold first saw Twickenham he was shocked by the dreadful state of the stadium and totally perplexed by the workforce that the Hales had assembled. In his enjoyable memoirs that are housed in the World Rugby Museum, Clark lays bare the failings he witnessed.

> I realised what a tip the whole place was. The ground staff mess turned out to be an old urinal with seats all around. On the floor were several men laid with coats over them asleep. I realised they were drunk. I asked Sidney Hale who they were and he told me they were part of my staff. It was usual for the ground staff to steal beer before any match when it was on the premises. I just could not believe this but it was perfectly true and I found out later that the ground staff stole beer and hid it in ovens, wellington boots, behind girders etc.

This scene of chaos had a profound effect on Clark, who had previously spent many years working at Castle Howard, the stunning stately home of the Howard family that would provide the backdrop for the 1981 ITV series *Brideshead Revisted*. Did Clark really want to swap the tranquil beauty of the Howardian Hills for a position that put him in charge of a bunch of drunks whose main motivation appeared to be finding new hiding places for stolen beer? (When manhole covers were later lifted for inspection, bottles of beer were found stacked in every available space.) Patently, the

Twickenham hierarchy must have recognised the seriousness of the situation by inviting Clark to take over. The unacceptable working practices might have continued for years if Clark had not been persuaded that the job of Twickenham Stadium's first clerk of works was not a poisoned chalice. He had severe doubts and made these clear to the Union's top brass. 'I wrote and told Mr Prescott [the secretary of the RFU] that I had changed my mind and didn't want the job. I realised the whole place was quite a "dump" and the playing area was ankle deep in mud. It seemed the head groundsman had been sacked because he had been selling material and spent most of his time at the public house and – unfortunately – was an alcoholic. He even sold the dandelions in the car park to children with rabbits.'

When Clark arrived there were twelve ground staff and he immediately appointed Malcolm Werret as groundsman, who replaced Les Hunt. Clark never lost a match to the weather in eighteen years and the instigation of his new sand-slitting process meant that from 1965 until his retirement, he put 1,680 tonnes of sand from Leighton Buzzard into the playing area.

John Clark remembers his father's dismay at the state of the home of English rugby and said, 'Twickenham was an absolute tip when my father arrived and he did a really good job during his time at the stadium. There were three Hale brothers who were sons of Charlie who laid the pitch. They used to top-dress the pitch along the sides where the scrums took place and you could put a bucket in the middle of the pitch and not see it from either side because it had been built up so much. Harlequins played eighteen matches a season and it all got impacted and there was no one there who knew about looking after the pitch.'

Harold kept the length of the Twickenham grass at around three to four inches, which often surprised visiting teams more used to shorter pitches, but the clerk of works had to guard against the ever-present threat of frost. Up to twenty tons of straw was spread over the pitch to combat heavy frost, and it usually took the ground staff two days to put this rather rustic protection in place. However, after doing its job it had to be quickly taken off, with three hours the preferred timescale if enough willing hands and pitch-forks were available.

Under the North Terrace Harold cleared away the mess that had been allowed to collect for decades and installed sliding doors with workshops behind, including storerooms for everything from grass seed to toilet rolls. The machines to keep the pitch in shape were also housed in this area, while a joinery shop enabled the ground staff to make new flip-up wooden seats to replace those that had been damaged during matches. The staff of twelve also made all the painted signs that were displayed around the stadium. The old urinal he was offered as a base was eventually swapped for a proper mess for the staff in the old joinery shop in the East Stand.

Harold Clark didn't suffer fools or badly behaved supporters gladly and this was apparent from his very first season in charge of the stadium. His son John not only remembers his father's love for the job but also his ability to hand out summary justice to those who deserved it. Clark senior's first home match with France was a 9–6 win for England in 1965. While escorting visiting fans along the front of the West Stand his bowler hat was knocked off, and as he bent down to pick it up he was kneed in the backside by one of the fans. Harold, a big man, felled the fan with a single punch – he escaped punishment as there were, quite obviously, extenuating circumstances. He tackled a flag seller who was operating illegally outside the stadium before another match and the irate salesman punched him on the jaw. Then there was the violent man at a UAU (Universities Athletic Union) match who was held by Harold over a barrier until the police arrived. Harold was also on hand in 1974 when future Cabinet minister Peter Hain, who was protesting against the Lions tour to South Africa, came down from his demonstration on top of the Twickenham ticket office roof. The clerk of works told Hain his fortune while holding him by the lapels!

Living on site in the cottage that would be knocked down when the North Stand was replaced meant the Clark family were always on hand to deal with problems, and one of them was reported to Harold by his daughter's boyfriend. The young man insisted there was a cat trapped in the stadium and it was meowing loudly. Harold had to open up the gates, which had been closed sometime earlier following a game with Ireland. Entering the stand, he didn't discover a cat – instead, there, forlornly calling out in a drunken stupor, was an Irish fan who had been left behind by his mates.

Boisterous, beer-fuelled supporters would cause Harold endless headaches and he became so irritated by those fans who used to climb into the steel supports above the South Terrace bar and strip off their clothes that he used black paint that never dried to cover the perching areas on the girders and trusses. In January 1966, his first England vs Wales game (won by Wales 11–6), the crowd used stacked-up straw bales to break down the east car park fence and then swarmed into the ground – this stadium boundary was replaced with steel fencing. That match also suffered a power cut in a distribution box near the stadium. Inside the ground, the fans were causing more mayhem in the gloom. Harold remembered the crowd lighting fires in the bars and waste-paper baskets to create light as they continued drinking, and the only way to clear the area was to ask the police to run through the crowd on motor bikes.

When Harold arrived he had found 156 public water closets that were rusting away, while the bowls used in the bars to clean the glasses were wooden and had to be kept filled with water to stop them cracking when not in use. Everything had to be replaced and updated, including installing a long trough-style urinal in the South Terrace area. During this period, the stadium boasted five permanent restaurants along with mobile canteens and twenty bars, with another twelve takeaway drinks bars installed on match days. Ring & Brymer had enjoyed the Twickenham concession for food and drinks from 1926 and, tired of replacing their entire stock of glass pints due to breakages, they introduced plastic ones – producing 10,000 with handles – only for these to disappear, taken as souvenirs of a Twickenham day out. In 1974–75 the RFU brought in restrictions to the drinking time of fans, with the bars shutting fifteen minutes before kick-off, remaining shut during the match and closing for a good hour after the final whistle.

The first clerk of work's time in charge saw a number of

thefts from the stadium, with many of those involved caught and brought to justice. The lead was stripped from the west restaurant porch roofs; the thief was seen and stopped on his bike and got six months in jail. A clerk from the ticket office, according to Harold's memoirs, was found to be stealing tickets and selling them for £20, and he also received six months in prison. The ground staff were also distracted by the appearance of nude women on the pitch who were taking part in a photographic shoot that one of the assistant secretaries had arranged without checking what kind of clothing (if any) the models would be wearing. The sights the staff saw peering through various gates proved to be the only record of the shoot as the RFU banned the pictures from being published once they discovered what kind of session they had allowed on the hallowed turf.

The stadium work continued under Harold's direction and the RFU would eventually be given the very first UK ground safety certificate after £600,000 of work had been carried out. The licence they received was No. 001. Twickenham's original set of rugby posts had been presented to Rugby School in 1956 and a new pair installed, made from ships' masts, with the staff taking, according to Wallace Reyburn in his book, 'an hour to put up the posts and an hour and a half to take them down'. The crossbars were removed during the 1969 Springbok tour due to the threat of protesters breaking into the ground and stealing them. On one occasion the south end crossbar was stolen and left in the garden of a house in Palmerston Road opposite No. 5 gate. A wagon picked it up but it wasn't returned to the RFU until six months later!

Not surprisingly, Harold's reputation spread around the world and he was offered the chance to look after all the grass grounds in Saudi Arabia for very impressive salary of £40,000. But the man who had painted in large letters 'TWICKENHAM' on the East Stand roof, a name that was seen by hundreds of thousands of air passengers over the years as they peered out of aircraft windows on the approach to Heathrow, could not leave his beloved stadium. And when it was time for this larger-than-life character to retire, the family name would continue to be associated with Twickenham.

When Harold ended his period in charge of the stadium the handover was made considerably easier for all concerned when the RFU appointed his son John to the role, and for an interim handover period at the start of 1982 both men were running the place. John had lived in the cottage on site ever since his father had taken up the position and, although he had established his own career path, the chance to apply for a job he knew so well appeared a natural option. 'I am a joiner by trade and worked for Costain, then the Property Services Agency. I got a call from Richmond College and they wondered if I fancied teaching. My wife, Jane, asked if she should bin the application form which she found in the house, but I applied for the Construction and Design Centre and they offered me the job there and then. So I took it and stayed for seven years. The Twickenham job as clerk of works was advertised nationally when my father finished and I applied for the post and so did my brother-in-law! For some reason they gave it to me and my father was under-standably delighted. They had just built the South Stand at the stadium and my first game as clerk of works was England versus Australia when Erica Roe did her famous streak.'

Thanks to the work his father had undertaken, John took over a stadium that was light years away from the 'mad house' Harold had described to his son after visiting Twickenham before he accepted the job in 1964. John would stay in the post for twenty-six years, taking control of the stadium and the pitch during the rebuilding period that would transform Twickenham into a modern arena.

'I had a team of ground staff and everyone mucked in when we needed the pitch covered or sand-slitting until Keith Kent arrived as head groundsman,' said John Clark. 'During my time the pitch used to fall about a foot east to west after we laser-levelled it in the early 2000s. The north car park flooded twice during my time at Twickenham and came up to the doorstep on one occasion at the cottage where we lived.' One of the peculiar aspects of playing at Twickenham before the arrival of the new stands was the need for the players to walk up steps to get to the pitch, but that is no longer the case. 'The pitch height hasn't changed, just the stands have changed. There also used to be a little fence on the east and west sides around the pitch which players had to avoid. When we dug up the southeast corner we brought up a piece of concrete that had obviously been a path alongside a greenhouse when the area had been orchards and market gardens and it had a groove that was a gutter.'

The RFU didn't know it, but they had chosen a man with a head for heights when they appointed John Clark, which would come in handy as the new North Stand towered over everything else in the area. After the first of the cantilever supports was put into the ground to create the first steel truss to hold up the roof, John took the opportunity to get a bird's-eye view of the pitch that had become his responsibility eight years earlier. With just thin wire running along the length of the truss to act as a safety rail, John walked out onto that single piece of steel. 'When they put the first steel truss out it was thirty-nine metres long and it was on its own. For the fun of it I walked out to the end of it and you do silly things at times. You look down and there is nothing – which does make your feet sweat a bit – but it wasn't too bad. Two of us went out, one of the chaps from Mowlem's joined me and we didn't use a safety rope, there was just a rail along the sides.' Happily, John and his companion returned safely from their hair-raising jaunt, one that up to this day had remained his own little secret. Terry Ward, the stadium architect, believes John was 120 feet above the pitch at the end of that truss and very few people at Twickenham at that time would have volunteered to join him. Having been part of a small group of press and RFU officials present for the topping-off of the North Stand, which involved travelling up rickety ladders tied together, I cannot comprehend the nerve it must have taken for John to walk out onto that single piece of steel.

Travelling to the top of the completed North Stand would be a regular occurrence during his time in charge, with John having the responsibility of collecting the Royal Standard from Buckingham Palace that flew from one of the flagpoles on top of the stand whenever the Queen visited the stadium. The flagpole is reached by a circuitous route and you need to know your way around the cavernous interior of the stand. Once outside, there are handrails guiding you around the entire roof – if you want to make the journey – and John reports the views are spectacular. Back on land, John threw himself into the many jobs that came under the remit of the clerk of works during his time at Twickenham. These included having the lion that stands on top of the Rowland Hill Gates covered in gold leaf in time for the 1991 Rugby World Cup, the final of which was staged at Twickenham – the 24-carat gold is expected to last for thirty years.

What many fans do not realise when they visit the stadium for a match is that, while they are sitting in their seats enjoying the spectacle, an army of workers swings into action before and after half-time. Not surprisingly, 82,000 people create a lot of mess both inside and outside the many toilets that are now on offer to visitors. Marshalling the required army of workers was one of John's key roles and he operated a 'scree list'.

He explained: 'Before the match I had a scree for everyone listing all that needed to be done by ground staff and it included cleaning the stadium and toilets during the match and after the fans had gone home. It used to cost around forty-five to fifty pence a head [for 82,000 fans] to clean the stadium but when the costs came in people would still ask, "Do we have to do this or that?" without understanding how important the cleaning was to produce a stadium that was ready for fans both at the start of the game, at half-time when they poured back into the bars, toilets and food outlets, and also to clear up after everyone had gone home. In recent years we did start cleaning as soon as the whistle sounded the start of the match. Cleaners would be out on the concourses picking up litter so that it was clean when they [the fans] came out at half-time to get more drink and food; and that process would start again when the second half was being played. That meant that when the game finished it was clean for the fans. In my father's day the fans would have been knee-deep in rubbish. When it was Middlesex Sevens day I would look at the stands and wonder how people got into their seats, there was so much rubbish around. It was an incredible sight. In the bars, the switch to plastic pints was logical because the glass ones that had been supplied by Ring & Brymer were constantly smashed and the cost of replacement must have been horrendous.'

One of the most popular Twickenham pastimes for fans who arrived by car was to set up a picnic in one of the car parks and bring out a barbecue to cook lunch. This is a tradition that has, unfortunately, been ended by health and safety rules, as it was pointed out that having flames right next to petrol tanks was asking for trouble. In fact, there were no real problems ever recorded in the Twickenham car parks, although John did witness one owner who took catering to the absolute limits. 'The barbecue was very much part of the pre-match occasion but the local authority were not very keen on all of these fires next to cars. I did see a barbecue set up in a car boot patently on top of the petrol tank – unbelievable. But there were never any serious problems for us.'

John's time in charge did not involve the kind of problems with staff that his father had wrestled with when temptation, in the form of food and beer, was left lying around, but he remembers what it was like when Harold took over. 'When the catering company would leave after a match there would be surplus food in the restaurants, beer in the bars – all bottled – and some of the ground staff would come in on the Monday and the first thing they did was raid the bars. You used to pull up manhole covers and find bottles stacked in there. Others tied string to the bottles and dropped them down behind the steel webbing so they could be drunk on a regular basis. I remember the old North Stand was a disgrace because under the stands there was wire netting keeping the public away from a load of junk, some of which must have been there since the stand was built. By creating shops for tradesmen it was a chance to knock the place into shape.'

John has vivid memories of the fans being equally committed to getting hold of as much drink as possible before, during and most notably after Twickenham matches. Certain 'hot spots' attracted revellers who thought nothing of climbing onto various roofs and sliding down into the arms of their friends. 'I can remember people in the west park bar area getting into the water storage tanks and chucking water over everyone. People on the roof were running down and diving into the concourse area where their mates would catch them – it really was amazing. They weren't hooligans – they were people who had been out for a session and they would just chuck pint glasses around and go and get another one when they needed a drink. It used to take a week for the ground staff to clean up – between their own drinks – and then it was a case of preparing for the Middlesex Sevens. There was never a need for a huge police presence at Twickenham. While the fans are a lively lot, there weren't any serious problems during my time. The police did have a room at the north end of the East Stand where unruly fans could be taken to cool down. The spectators at Twickenham do regulate themselves and it really was a brilliant place on match days without any real trouble, and that continues to be the case today.'

The Sevens has a legendary reputation for all-day drinking by rugby fans and the ticket office would issue 10,000 fewer tickets than the stadium capacity to allow for movement, particularly when the terraces were still in operation at Twickenham. 'They used to sell Party Seven large cans at that time and after the tournament there would be a mountain of these in the north car park waiting for the council to come and collect them. I remember that one team used to carry into the ground a barrel of beer along with a gas bottle and set up a working beer pump on the North Terrace with a tap on the fence so they could pull pints all day. It was quite a place.'

Unfortunately, what goes in has to come out and for those fans who used to watch Twickenham matches in the upper North Stand, that meant peeing where they could find a wall. This had a cumulative effect on the structure as well as wetting those below. 'For many years we were trying to upgrade the toilets,' said John, 'because there was a lot of peeing going on in the North Stand and it was running down onto those below, which was very unpleasant, so we put urinals throughout the upper tiers. The North Stand was rebuilt for the 1991 World Cup and the council planners . . . I like to think I can get a smile out of most people even if it's out of sympathy – but I couldn't crack those guys.

They were awful. The mistake we made with the North was trying to open it in too many different phases and it was a bit of a nightmare getting the safety certificate with one not being given until noon on the Saturday of the match.'

Suddenly, from a stadium clad in asbestos sheeting with staircases linking different levels, John was overseeing the use of a modern stadium made of concrete and steel with escalators, lifts, air-conditioning units and all kinds of power-hungry items, particularly in the new kitchens set up to feed the thousands now taking advantage of the burgeoning corporate hospitality market. The West Stand contains the biggest of Twickenham's kitchens, next to the Spirit of Rugby restaurant. The arrival of the digital age also ended a family tradition in the Clark household, with the match score being displayed electronically. For many years, together with his wife and children, John would make the perilous journey over the edge of the old West Stand upper tier and climb through a trapdoor in the roof of the scoreboard, featuring numbers placed in grooves. The family would then put up the scores of the different matches – not internationals – from their vantage point hanging off the front of the stand.

With the increase in power demand came the need to install backup generators; Twickenham can supply its needs from standby, on-site generators in case the mains supply is lost. The television companies also bring their own backup in case of emergency, while there are always experts on call on match days within the stadium to solve any problems that arise. 'We ran the new scoreboards off generators and we always knew that if there was a power loss we had emergency lighting and the generators as backup to finish the match and then it would be a case of getting everyone home. We had people ready on site to repair lifts and escalators and other areas and you would take criticism when they weren't needed because nothing had failed during a match. People would say, "Can't you just ring them up if something goes wrong?" without understanding the problems of moving around the area on match day. I used to think, are they nuts, we have 82,000 fans on site!'

One group of visitors was always welcome: the Jehovah's Witnesses who held their annual convention in the stadium and have been regulars for sixty years. What impressed both father and son in the Clark household was the tidiness of the church members, who cleaned up after every convention – unlike rugby fans. 'They used to tie signs onto everything and left a long piece of string on a drain pipe outside the dressing room, and Albert Agar, the former president, walked past, looked up and turned to me and said, "This place is tied up with string." Besides their sign-making, the Witnesses also baked and cooked on site.'

Moves that appear to the outsider merely cosmetic, but had a significant effect on the way the grounds were able to be developed, also took place during John's period in charge. There used to be allotments around the northern fringe of the stadium and these had to be relocated (with financial compensation thrown into the equation) to open up the area for both the car-parking requirements and the expansion of the television area where the scanner vehicles and power-generation units are parked. With the increase in car numbers – there are spaces for nearly 4,000 today – utilising the Cardinal Vaughan school playing fields (which are operated on a long-term lease) became a real issue. Once again, John came up with a solution, and one that ensures easy access for all concerned. 'We had to move some of the allotments and that was a dour affair, and I left a little bit of space between Chase Bridge School and the allotments thinking that one day we may go on to Cardinal Vaughan and we may need a bridge. We did eventually build one – after initially putting in a prefab one for the matches.'

John Clark's memories of his time at Twickenham are framed by smiles as he recalls incidents that at the time were far from funny but now, with hindsight, get him chuckling. One of the strongest images he has is of a broken-down Land Rover standing in the middle of the pitch in 1986 in the hours before England were due to play Ireland. The game was under real threat of being postponed due to heavy frost and snow affecting the whole country, and one of the key instructions given to Twickenham ground staff was to ensure that all motorised equipment, particularly on match days, was always topped up with fuel. It transpired that the Land Rover had an empty tank, not a mechanical problem, which made RFU officials even more irate.

John said, 'There were straw sheds in two areas of the ground and they were always full. I never put on straw but we did use pitch covers; however there was a very long cold spell which meant the pitch set hard for the three weeks leading up to that match. I told the groundsman we had to do something about the rock-hard surface and we bought a scaffold frame and put tarpaulins over a 30-metre area and put space heaters under them and ran the system twenty-four hours a day for a week, and banked areas that had been treated with double covers to keep the heat in. The west side was worse than the east and we got the whole pitch thawed out by about 1 a.m. on the Saturday morning – match day. The teams were happy to play on the pitch and so we headed off to sleep, with some of the workers sleeping in the dressing rooms. At 5 a.m. Ken Cox, who was in charge of the dressing rooms, knocked on the cottage door and said, "Come and have a look at this."

'There was an inch and a half of snow all over the stadium. We got a long-wheel-based Land Rover and a truck to move the collected snow because I didn't want to put the tractor on the covers – which were blanketed in snow – that were protecting the pitch. But we had to clear the covers to get them off the pitch. You would never get away with this today, but our answer was to drive the Land Rover onto the pitch and we started filling the truck with snow and taking it off to the north car park. We had a guy called Reg, a mechanic, who we used to tell to just make sure all the kit was working for match day. He came across to me and I could see he wasn't happy. He told me the Land Rover had run out of petrol and was now stuck in the middle of the pitch. Assistant Sec. Colonel Dennis Morgan went scarlet.'

With time running out to save the match, John found himself with one of his vehicles immobile on the pitch and the nearest petrol some distance away in the snow. Needing inspiration, John walked out of the stadium and into the west car park, which had just opened to allow those fans with car-park passes to set up their barbecues and bars for the famous pre-international parties. Thankfully, one of the earliest arrivals had travelled through the snow in his own Land Rover. 'We went into the car park and found a chap with a Land Rover and he drove onto the pitch and towed our vehicle and trailer off. Eventually we got all the snow from the covers and referee Clive Norling wanted the in-goal areas shortened and we rolled the covers up and left them at either end. After the covers came off we realised the pitch had not been marked and so we got that finished just as Clive blew the whistle to start the match.'

One thing that would have helped John immensely on days like that was undersoil heating, something that would be not installed until the new £1.25m Desso pitch was put in under the watchful eye of Keith Kent, the current head groundsman. Kent explained: 'We put undersoil heating in during 2012 and we can now use it. It's hot-water pipes that went in under the Desso pitch. You put stone in, then six inches of sand, then pull the pipes in and then put a top four inches of roots so you have ten inches of root zone for the Desso. We have sensors in the ground and also one above the pitch and the heating is set to come on at plus-three Celsius. That is usually zero on the grass, and the colder it gets the warmer the water gets to combat the frost. We have covers we can put on to combat snow on the pitch and, being a 28-acre site, it's also about the snow in all the other areas. The pitch will always be OK but it could be problems with health and safety in the stadium.'

Kent increases the available heat on the pitch with the use of lighting rigs that promote grass growth and negate the lack of natural sunlight, particularly at the south end of the stadium. However, this also attracts foxes, who know the area is going to offer a warm bed for the night in winter. Unfortunately, they also bring food with them which leads to strange discoveries in various areas of the pitch – most notably the holes where the posts are erected. Ground staff have pulled out plastic bags containing sausages the foxes have managed to steal from the nearby Tesco supermarket while, on one occasion, they found a dead pigeon only half-buried in the turf by a fox. It was easily spotted as the dead bird's backside was sticking out of the grass. The RSPCA are called in when there is a serious fox problem, while a hawk is employed to keep pigeons out of the stadium, reducing the amount of droppings and seed stealing. Kent said, 'Lighting rigs are another way of battling the elements – with a wrapa-round stadium we get very little sunshine in the stadium because it can't get over the South Stand. That is why we use the rigs to give every area the light it needs, and it keeps it alive from the end of September until the start of March. You do get families of foxes because it's a minimum of three degrees warmer under the lamps, and we put scarers in to try and move them on. Whenever we seed the pitch we bring in a hawk but the pigeons are not daft and come back in the evening to eat when the hawk's gone.'

Birds have been a long-standing problem at Twickenham. Harold Clark reported that, during his time as clerk of works in the 1960s, he called back the painting company that had given the stadium a new look when he discovered that the lazy contractors had merely painted over the 'two inches of pigeon droppings' that had accumulated on the steel struts of the stadium. Neither Harold nor the company tasked with the job were amused and those responsible were let go. The RSPCA also mounts cockerel patrols for games with France as the visiting fans like nothing better than to announce their arrival by throwing a live cockerel onto the Twickenham pitch.

It was entirely appropriate that when John ended his twenty-six years as clerk of works – bringing to a conclusion a family involvement with the stadium that stretched over the most important years of Twickenham's evolution – he was able to mark the occasion on top of the North Stand. This time he wasn't perched on a single steel truss 120-feet up, but standing alongside one of the flagpoles. On match days, flags of the competing nations join the Union Jack in flying from the top of the North Stand and it was here that John had the honour of raising the London Olympic flag on his last day in post on 24 August 2008. As he recalled: 'All major sporting [stadia] were raising the Olympic flag and Richard Prescott, RFU head of communications, said, "The old boy is clearing off, let him do it!" It was a lovely honour and I raised it on the North Stand roof – a place I have been hundreds of times. To get there, you go up to level six in the North Stand and there is a ladder into the lift motor room and the walkway goes out onto a gangway and all around the roof of the stadium. It is a different world up there, with fantastic views. You can even see the Houses of Parliament.'

The London 2012 flag was raised above the home of England Rugby to mark the handover of the Olympic Flag to Mayor of London Boris Johnson during the closing ceremony of the Beijing Games. The flag flew strongly in the wind and John was totally untroubled by the blustery conditions high up above the pitch his family had worked so hard to tend. Clark volunteered to be a Games Maker during the Olympics and as a cycling enthusiast was delighted to be assigned to the velodrome, where he witnessed many of Great Britain's medal-winning rides, enjoying a different world-class sporting arena for a change. As he reflected on a long family involvement with Twickenham, John only had one regret: 'I wanted the concourses closed in on the upper levels because it can get really cold up there and it would have been nice if I could have done that before leaving. Overall, I don't think we did a bad job and turned out a pretty good stadium. I shall always have special memories of Twickenham and be proud of it, but it is someone else's ground now. Dad died at the age of ninety-six and used to go to the matches after he retired – we both loved the place.' At the end of his tenure, the long Clark family involvement with Twickenham ended, but their legacy lives on.

It was the increased use of the Twickenham pitch that forced the RFU and head groundsman Keith Kent to opt for a different kind of surface. A purely grass pitch would not have allowed so many matches to be played at Twickenham and that is why plastic became the best option. Kent came to Twickenham in 2002 after spending fifteen years ensuring the Old Trafford pitch offered Manchester United the best possible surface for some of the world's leading football players. Kent had little knowledge of rugby but was ready for a new challenge and was fired by the myriad uses being planned for the sport's most iconic stadium. 'The biggest consideration when I was thinking of leaving Manchester United to join the RFU was that having been in football all of those years, all I had ever done was football, and you are only in this life once! I know absolutely nothing about rugby having played, at most, three games at school, and while I don't understand all the rules, I do love watching the Six Nations on the TV. I came for my interview with [stadium director] Richard Knight and we sat around with a cup of coffee. Richard said the new South Stand was going to be built at Twickenham with the hotel making it a wrap-around stadium, and that was something I was used to at Old Trafford. He said that Twickenham wanted to host rock and roll concerts and I would be able to help with those. Man United's Old Trafford pitch would be used for up to sixty games during a season and we open the Twickenham gates twenty-one times a year and play up to fifty games. People won't realise there are that many matches and for example: on the day of the England versus Barbarians at the start of June, that is just one of four matches being played on that day on the pitch. The day before is the Aviva Premiership final, and you just wouldn't get that in football. '

The Desso pitch was installed in 2012 and replaced a surface that was starting to show its age. With the 2015 Rugby World Cup on the horizon, everyone at the stadium knew something had to be done to ensure the pitch could handle the demands of the tournament. Putting in a new pitch meant that the drop from west to east could be adjusted, although there is still a natural flow of drainage with a smaller drop. However, the days when you could stand a bucket in the middle of the pitch and not be able to see it are a distant memory.

'There is only a drop of seven inches from one side to another,' said Kent, 'and when I took over it was a fibre sand pitch which had been laid in 2000 with five-metre drain and one-metre sand slits and the rest was 1910 allotments soil on the base. When I first arrived the pitch hadn't got the kind of care that Old Trafford had received in terms of fertilising and the grass was too long. I increased the fertiliser regime and cut the grass shorter. Having met Clive Woodward on my second day in the job I asked him, "What do you want to play on?" and he said a fast track. We took it down to 35–40mm that first season when it had been 50–60mm.' After several years in the job Kent realised the pitch needed another overhaul. 'I sat down with Richard Knight and said the pitch was getting older and by the time we started looking for a new one it was nearly eleven years old. The drainage had started to slow down to about 15mm an hour and if we had suffered a thunderstorm on a match day we would have been struggling. I said that we needed a new pitch for the World Cup in 2015 and he tasked me with going out and finding the right one. I had seen Desso a long, long time ago in football and I travelled the country to try and find something better.

'There was a new product out called fibre elastic which was a step up from fibre sand. I visited Newcastle United and their pitch was perfect. I went to Glasgow Rangers and because the drainage was so good, the surface was drying out. I came to the conclusion that with four games over a short period, my pitch would get too dry and they would be kicking it to death. So I discarded the idea of fibre elastic and we went down the Desso road. It is a magnificent product; we can drain at 122mm an hour. We put irrigation on overnight to ensure the grass is dry because the players like that to help with handling, but the sand underneath will still be damp.'

Installing a Desso pitch does not mean the surface can then be viewed as artificial or plastic. While 48,000 kilometres of material has been woven into the Twickenham turf, it only constitutes 3 per cent of the pitch. 'That's right. Only 3 per cent of the pitch is artificial and they put in a strand of artificial grass that goes in a loop eight inches deep and is 20mm above the surface of the grass and being green it cannot be seen. There is a strand of grass in a loop every 20mm across the entire surface, which means we have 48,000km of the artificial strand in the pitch, enough to go around the world with a bow on top! A Desso pitch can last ten years but Huddersfield Town had one of the first pitches and they play football and rugby league on it and it lasted thirteen seasons, while West Ham still play on theirs which is around twelve years old.'

Kent explained that the great strengths of the Desso system were its stability and quick draining. 'You cannot kick a divot out of the pitch. Circulation of air is important and in a bowl it can appear like a woodland glade, which is great for growing mushrooms. You can come in on a morning and if it's been heavy dew it looks like a frost, but that increases the chance of disease and so we do have to remove that water. We tried at old Trafford with about a dozen electric fans, which make a lot of noise and after about twenty yards the air started to dissipate. [Here] we pull a rope across the pitch to knock the dew off or we brush it.'

When the South Stand was built, architect Terry Ward ensured the circulation of air would remain 'healthy' for the pitch, despite not being able to create the same number of 'vomitories' that feature in the other three stands. These are, basically, open windows with the air able to rush through the openings into the stadium. With a hotel as part of the development at the south end, this was not going to be possible. Ward's answer was to install motorised 'blades' that can be opened and shut, depending on the need for air movement, as he explained: 'The quality of the pitch was one of the reasons a roof was never really considered and they have never had problems with the turf at Twickenham apart from the northwest corner where the sun didn't really get to that area as much as other parts. Daylight and air movement are vital and we have not wrapped Twickenham in an external wall for those reasons, and that is why we have the middle and upper tiers open allowing wind to get in through the vomitories. On the lower level, the wind can also move in and out in the corners to ensure air movement for the grass and I think this is one of the secrets of Twickenham's success. When we built the South Stand we put movers at the top to allow more air into the stadium – blades that can be opened and shut at the back of the upper tier.'

The introduction of 3G fully artificial pitches at Saracens and Cardiff rugby clubs are the latest and, many would argue, inevitable development for sports pitches in this country, where poor weather for winter sports is a crucial factor. Saracens can play numerous games during the day on the pitch without damage being sustained. Snow is removed using a tractor with a large brush on the front, and the 3G has been so well received that the 2014 Amlin Challenge Cup final was played on the surface when the match was given to Cardiff Blues to stage at the Arms Park. Kent acknowledges the advantages of a fully artificial pitch but added, 'Artificial pitches have a place and you have to be pragmatic and they can train twenty-four hours a day without any damage, and my Desso pitch is like the hall carpet, it wears down the middle! Whatever you play on needs maintenance but I just wonder if we need to play competitive games on an artificial pitch, because it could possibly change the sport. Your heart is in your mouth when they are resetting scrum after scrum on the same area of a Desso pitch but where would the game be without the scrum?'

England's forensic approach to trying to become the number-one team in the world includes enlisting Kent's help to ensure their training pitch is as close to Twickenham as possible, and that means spending more time at Pennyhill Park, the five-star country hotel where England are based in the build-up to Test matches at Twickenham. They have a pitch within the grounds of the hotel and the RFU has built an indoor-training facility which does feature a plastic mini-pitch for when the weather is too poor for outdoor work. 'We are getting more and more involved with the pitch at Pennyhill Park where England train and you do want a similar surface. Manchester City had seven Desso pitches put into their training ground to mirror the Man City stadium. When he hired me Richard Knight said, "One of the things I would like you to do is travel around the country and offer advice and help to all the community clubs," and that was one of the hooks that got me. I can be at all the big games, against New Zealand and South Africa, and then the following week in Harrogate looking at pitches, or Northumbria, Cumbria or Kent. I enjoy meeting people and so it means I have the best of both worlds with the high-profile matches at Twickenham but also the contact with local rugby people talking about their own pitches and problems.

'My staff, Ian and Andy, are fabulous and I trust them implicitly and that means I can make those visits and be back on Friday knowing everything will be fine, and it's a fabulous life and way to make a living. I learn a lot about the volunteers in rugby and there are so many characters involved in the game that I have met over the last nine years. I enjoy passing on bits of information and the game is so traditional and well disciplined. The respect for the referee and coaches is incredible. You don't see anyone feigning injury and rolling about.'

Chapter Six

Twickenham Stadium and the
two World Wars

There are two wooden plaques near the entrance to the RFU Members' Lounge in the West Stand at Twickenham that pay tribute to those English internationals who lost their lives in the First and Second World Wars. Of the thirty players who appeared in the 1914 England vs Scotland match, eleven were killed in the conflict that followed.

The effect on the stadium of the two conflicts was minimal, despite the Blitz on London in the Second World War. King George V unveiled a war memorial to the dead of the First World War at Twickenham in 1921, and that brass plaque is now found in the West Stand foyer on the wall near the lifts, along with the plaque produced for those who fell in the Second World War. The centenary of the RFU in 1971 is also commemorated.

During the First World War, the pitch was used to graze horses and farm animals as it was still very much part of the rural landscape of the Twickenham area. The Great War broke out just seven years after the land had been bought and the stadium was still in its formative period. The Second World War had a far more dramatic influence on the life of the stadium, which did not host any matches for the duration of the conflict. The practice of chopping and storing wood under the South Terrace during the war led to an infestation of rats. That was in stark contrast to the rest of the stadium, which became home to the local Civil Defence units, who stripped the changing rooms and turned them into casualty stations to deal with the threat of chemical attack. Anti-gas equipment was installed in the changing rooms and the West Stand restaurant was turned into a medical post with beds and nurses on duty to deal with potential victims. The new pavilion, constructed in 1937 with the RFU accepting the lowest tender of £9,941, was also available for war use.

The east car park was dug up for allotments while the west car park became a massive coal dump; other areas became parking for army trucks and firefighting equipment. The only reported hit by a German bomb came on 1 July 1944 when a V-bomb landed on Talma Gardens, with the West Stand sustaining some damage. The major problem created for the stadium by the Blitz on London was caused by 'friendly fire' in the form of shrapnel which fell onto the stand roofs. This was the result of the anti-aircraft shells fired at German aircraft bombing the city, with the resulting shrapnel heading back to earth. The stadium was derequisitioned on 20 September 1945; during the six years of war, the only work that was undertaken was to cut the grass on the pitch. Rugby returned to the stadium on 24 November 1945 when an England XV played the New Zealand Army, and the Varsity Match was staged on 12 December. The upper West Stand was not used for some time because of the damage to the roof, which meant rain drenched those underneath; with post-war shortages of materials, it became a question of waiting in line for your turn for supplies. The RFU did seek compensation from government, with Wallace Reyburn stating in his book *Twickenham: the Story of a Rugby Ground*, 'The RFU's claim for £12,000 compensation for the results of requisition was settled at a compromise of £7,000 and a tremendous amount of work by the Twickenham staff on repairs, cleaning and painting had the ground returning to something like normality when the Internationals were resumed again in the 1946–7 season.'

Life at Twickenham before and after the Second World War was detailed for the RFU museum by Tom Prentice, son of Doug Prentice, who was secretary of the Union from 1947 to 1962. Tom recorded his memories in the form of a letter which is now safely housed in the museum, and he had particularly strong recollections of Sydney F. Coopper, who played most of his career for Blackheath, where he earned the nickname 'The Jumping Wing' thanks to the way he dived over the try line and opponents. He also won two caps for the Navy after his international career had finished, in 1909 and 1910. He served on the Devon Rugby Union committee from 1922 to 1923 as the Devonport Services representative. He preceded Tom's father as secretary of the RFU from 1924 until the end of the 1946–47 season and during the Second World War was one of only two RFU men who stayed to look after the stadium. He was credited with ensuring those who were occupying Twickenham were able to effectively utilise the facilities. Prentice recalled:

> The other was head groundsman Mr Charles Hale senior, and everyone else went off to join the forces. No work, repairs, maintenance and painting was done with only the grass being cut. Twickenham was used by Civil Defence as a decontamination area after possible chemical attack on London and the area was full of vehicles. The dressing rooms were stripped and anti-gas equipment was installed with only the pitch spared of use. Coopper stayed on an extra year after the war to help put things back in order. An advert for a new Secretary was posted in the summer of 1946 and so my father F.D. Prentice was asked if he could wait a year before taking up the post he had been elected to. Coopper loved Twickenham so much he took a room in Alf Wright's house for when he came up from his home in St Mawes. The staff in 1947 was F.D. Prentice, with assistants Alf Wright and George Young and an administrative secretary Les Rose. The first Lady Secretary, Mrs Potts, was appointed making five in the office. There were five on the ground staff;

Mr Hale plus his sons Sydney, Wilfred and Ronald and Mr Tom Brock making a staff of 10. The Secretary lived in South View when in office.

Tom Prentice was able to help paint the West Stand and pack up batches of tickets for sending out to the clubs for international matches. He reported that:

> . . . the roofs of the stands still had holes caused by anti-aircraft shells falling back down as shrapnel. The iron work was rusty. the crowd barriers weakened and woodwork and seats needing repair or replacement. Only those who lived through the War can recall the restrictions, rationing, contracts and licences and although we were left shattered and impoverished the RFU, like so many organisations, gradually recovered and can be justly proud of the policies adopted at the time and development of the game since.

The war periods were part of the stadium's evolution that would see considerable expenditure over forty-three years from the purchase of the land in 1907 for £5,572 12s 6d. By the end of the 1940s a total of £246,489 had been spent by the RFU to create their home at Twickenham Stadium.

Chapter Seven

Peter Hain and the mystery of the swastika

One of the great mysteries of Twickenham Stadium revolves around the 1969–70 South African rugby tour to the UK and Ireland. Peter Hain led a successful campaign to disrupt the tour and the matches attracted thousands of anti-apartheid protesters, some of whom made it onto the pitch. Hain himself was ejected from all four Twickenham games – Oxford University, London Counties, England and Barbarians – he attended during the tour, but despite masterminding anti-apartheid protests by the Stop the Seventy Tour group, the man who would go on to become the popular MP for Neath in 1991 (a position he holds to this day) and land the roles of Leader of the House of Commons and Secretary of State for Northern Ireland (among other posts) in the Labour Government, cannot help solve the mystery of how a swastika and the letters 'AA' were burned into the Twickenham pitch and 'Remember Sharpeville' was painted onto corrugated sheeting in the West Terrace in the lead-up to the England vs South Africa international on 20 December 1969. England triumphed 11–8 to record their first ever victory over the Springboks in a match which featured noisy anti-apartheid demonstrations.

The Nazi symbol was burned into the centre spot of the Twickenham pitch before the international with South Africa, and while the painted message about the Sharpeville Massacre, when police shot dead sixty-nine black people in 1960, became common knowledge, the swastika damage and the initials 'AA' in the turf – standing for Anti-Apartheid – remained unknown outside the Clark family cottage in the grounds of the stadium. Harold Clark, the clerk of works, understood how much coverage the damage to the pitch would give the protesters and took it upon himself to gather up as many grass cuttings as he could and spread them over the damaged area. He did such a good job that no one noticed the swastika or the letters during the game and he was able to fully restore the grass after attention had moved away from Twickenham. 'The Twickenham posts were taken down after every match in case they were cut down and searchlights were on the ground and the police had dogs patrolling for three months,' Clark recalls in his memoirs lodged in the Twickenham museum. 'But, "Remember Sharpeville" was written in paint on the West Terrace and a swastika about twenty metres across on the centre of the playing area. Cut grass was put over the swastika and it never made the press. Glue was used on locks at the ground but paraffin saved all but one of them. We also had magnets to pick up tacks around the posts at the ready.'

His son John, who would take over from his father as clerk of works, has vivid memories of the day the protesters damaged the pitch. 'My mother woke me up to go to work and pulled back the curtains and said, "Oh my God, they've been." They had painted "Remember Sharpeville" on the corrugated wall of the West Terrace and burned a swastika and the letters AA on the pitch on the centre spot. We spread grass cuttings around and no one was any the wiser about the swastikas. I think my father may have also used some dye to help minimise the damage.'

Hain, who led the Stop the Seventy Tour group, only learned of the swastika when interviewed for this book and said: 'The burning of a swastika onto the pitch must have been done by someone acting freelance. It is a good idea, but not something I knew about happening at Twickenham. It was a co-ordinated campaign, but people were doing their own thing which was actually better. The Twickenham events tended to be major occasions of protest but there were also demonstrations around the country. I travelled to Twickenham by train and I don't remember being recognised by rugby supporters. There were four matches at Twickenham and I was carried out from all of them! The Oxford University match was switched the night before and we got a call from a journalist I knew who worked for the *Evening News*, who said it was Twickenham at 3 p.m., and I called everyone on our list. Coaches came from all over the place and the West Stand was the only area opened. It was easier to corral us but then it also made it easier to focus your efforts. The police were sort of prepared even though this was the first match for them and first protest for us.'

The police presence, recorded on Pathé News film, was around 540 officers, and this would increase to 800 for the Counties match with another 50 added for the international with England. The largest police presence was used to control protests at the final match against the Barbarians when 2,300 police, according to Wallace Reyburn, were reported to be on duty at Twickenham – in stark contrast to the present day when crowd control is undertaken by stewards employed by the RFU.

'I had never been to Twickenham before and we bought tickets for the Oxford University game on the day and went in,' added Hain. 'I was a sports fanatic but most of the other protesters were not and so, for them, a game of rugby was probably new. The atmosphere was strange for everyone tried to get onto the pitch and was carried away wearing a polo-necked jumper. I was hauled out of the ground and told to "shove off". They were stopping anyone coming back into the stadium and there had been constant chanting and "Sieg Heils" at the Springboks to equate them with the Nazis. There was quite an aggressive response from other spectators to what we were doing but not as much reaction as the England international in December. At the Oxford game there was a pensioner called Bill Laithwaite who disguised himself as a match official and underneath he had the anti-apartheid initials which he displayed and was then grabbed having got onto the pitch at half-time. He had blood on his head and must have been knocked about a bit.'

Terry Cooper, the Press Association's long serving former rugby correspondent, remembers Laithwaite's appearance, recalling: 'He was dressed in blazer and shorts and headed towards the centre mark, where the kick-off was being prepared. He kicked referee, Mike Titcomb, hard in the shin before being taken off.'

For the Oxford players, the build-up to that opening fixture at Twickenham on 5 November was totally disrupted. They knew the match could not be staged at Iffley Road, their usual venue for fixtures, because of the open nature of the ground. The players were offered the chance to drop out of the match on political grounds but all opted to play. The Hon. Justice Sir Jeremy Cooke, who played in the match, remembers being asked to appear on television with Malcolm Muggeridge and former Wales international Wilf Wooller to discuss the contest prior to match day. The Oxford players, led by All Black scrum-half Chris Laidlaw, were only told they were heading to Twickenham on the morning of the match and demonstrators were already there when the team arrived at the stadium. The players heard chanting throughout the game from the protesters and Michael Heal, the Oxford full-back who kicked his side to a famous 6–3 win, recalls the jeers being drowned by cheers as an upset result became a real possibility.

After the match, the players assembled for the reception in the RFU Committee room in the stadium and the mounted Springbok head – the traditional offering from the touring team to opponents – was then handed over. The secrecy surrounding the game against Oxford University meant a normal match programme couldn't be produced and the team lists were handed out to spectators having been produced on a mimeographed sheet of foolscap, according to Wallace Reyburn.

The main aim of the protests was to put pressure on the government and sporting authorities to cancel the proposed South African cricket tour in 1970, following the Basil D'Oliveria controversy when he was stopped from joining the 1968–69 England tour to the Republic. Hain says, 'There were twenty-five matches on that Springbok rugby tour and I was only thrown out of the four Twickenham ones despite lots of people – including my constituents – insisting they had seen me carried out of many more tour games. I did go to Leicester but to my great frustration couldn't get into the match, probably because as the national co-ordinator I was recognisable. I did take part and speak at a march in Leicester and we held a rally outside Welford Road. I wasn't at Swansea where the protesters were very roughly treated; however, people claim to have carried me off the pitch! I had a dozen people who absolutely swore they had taken me off and that I had spoiled their Saturday afternoon but they were still going to vote for me. The first big set piece was the London Counties game at Twickenham and we were even better organised for the match with England at the stadium in the December, but so were the police.'

With the authorities starting to understand the nature of the anti-apartheid demonstrations, access to Twickenham became tougher for the protesters. However, they circumvented attempts to deny them tickets with various ruses. 'Tickets for the international were really hard to come by and you couldn't just buy them on the day. We had people who were South Africans who went to the South African embassy where you could purchase tickets and they also made their way to the Twickenham ticket office in the build-up to the match. One woman claimed to be a teacher with eighty South African schoolchildren in her care and so we had all these people gathering as many tickets [as possible] for us to get into the ground on match day and protest. The tickets were dished out in somebody's front room around the corner from the stadium on match day and we did get access to the ring seats in the lower East Stand.

'We had two protesters who practised running around my garden and handcuffing themselves to a broom handle and one of them did get onto the pitch and lock himself onto one of the posts. We had packets of black dye to throw onto the damp pitch and turn the Springbok players black. We also had smoke flares and the pictures from the match and television coverage featured this dramatic footage of the smoke from the flares billowing in the middle of the rugby international and it looked chaotic. I am accused of backing the throwing of tacks onto rugby pitches during the tour and that wasn't true. There was one incident that I heard about where a teacher from Bristol scattered tacks onto a pitch and I think he was a member of the Communist Party. I had no knowledge that he was going to do that and didn't approve of that kind of action because our objective was not to injure anyone and to adopt classic non-violent direct action to interrupt the matches. Later, I had to track that teacher down and get his address and he was called as a witness to my conspiracy trial so that he could confirm he did that on his own volition.'

The violence towards protesters that had happened in Swansea did not transfer to the home of English rugby, although Hain recognised a distinct change in attitude to demonstrators by the time the England international arrived on the tour schedule. Now, rather than helping hand protestors over to the police, sections of the crowd, particularly those sitting in the level above where the anti-apartheid supporters were gathered, showed their displeasure by throwing the chair cushions you could hire at Twickenham down onto those trying to get onto the pitch. Hain continued: 'We felt that tour was building towards the England versus South Africa international at Twickenham in December and our main objective was to stop the cricket tour by South Africa to England in 1970. We had started on the rugby tour very late in the September and the Oxford University game was early November. The security at Twickenham was getting tighter all the time and by that stage the rugby spectators were deeply angry with us and it changed from an attitude of just ignoring the demonstrators to this real resentment, and I remember being in the East Stand lower area with most of the protestors and we did try and get onto the pitch with some people achieving that aim in the England game. I didn't get onto the pitch and was grabbed before I climbed over and was then pushed back. We then had seat cushions thrown down on us from the rugby fans who were sitting in the level above and it was quite frightening to get these cushions raining down on you with real screams of hatred as if we were some kind of alien species.'

The end of the 1969–70 Springbok tour did not signal the end of Hain's protests over sporting links with South Africa, and rugby maintained contact for many years to come. England arranged a Test with South Africa in Johannesburg in 1972 (which they would win, to the astonishment of the rest of the sport) and this also became a target for Hain's protest movement as they disrupted a training session at Richmond. Hain had written on a number of occasions to the RFU about the visit: 'I sent letters and did get replies but never had any conversations because, I suppose, it was war! It was impossible to stop teams going to South Africa but we had a good go at stopping the England team coach from taking the players from their Richmond hotel to Heathrow airport. We arranged for the fire brigade to turn up in front of the hotel and also ordered skips to be delivered.'

In 1974, the British and Irish Lions prepared for what turned out to be an unbeaten and record-breaking four-Test tour of South Africa. In an effort to gain publicity for their protests against the tour, Peter Hain and the anti-apartheid movement again focused on Twickenham Stadium. This time, rather than attempting to gain entry to the ground – there was nothing happening there at the time – Hain and two others got onto the Twickenham Stadium ticket office roof and let the press know they were there. Harold Clark, a man who never shrank away from confrontation when it involved someone messing around with his stadium, came up with a simple ruse to deal with Hain and his pals – he removed the ladder! Hain was on the roof for more than two hours before police put the ladders back and allowed the protesters to come down to where Clark was waiting. In his memoirs, Clark says he grabbed Hain by the lapels and enjoyed 'telling him his fortune'.

Hain has a clear memory of the protest and believes Clark's decision to take away the ladder actually helped prolong the incident rather than cause him any anguish. 'We were trying to get them to change their minds about the tour and I did have a face-to-face meeting with the captain, Willie John McBride, at one point but they were determined to go. We had a particularly resourceful member of the protest group, which included trade unionists, who recced the area and got the ladder. All I did was join that group and be the public figure for the press and there were pictures in that day's *Evening Standard* of us on the roof of the old ticket office. I can vaguely remember angry RFU officials after we came down. It didn't register as an ugly incident but, in effect, they played into our hands by taking the ladder away!'

Hain, whose campaign did force the cancellation of the 1970 South African cricket tour to England and initiated a much wider ban on sporting contacts with that country, did not return to Twickenham for more than twenty years. 'I never went back to the old Twickenham where we had held the protests and by the time I did return it was now around 1998 for an England–Wales game. The stadium was completely different with the horseshoe shape and I enjoyed some hospitality before the game. That international at Twickenham was the first time I was able to sit through a match there without being carried out!

'Looking back on the protests in 1969, if the rugby

authorities had switched that Oxford University match anywhere else rather than Twickenham Stadium, it would have made it much more difficult for us to get people there and the profile would have been much lower. From that moment, Twickenham Stadium became the magnet for demonstrators because it was London and the headquarters of English rugby. It was very much the focal point of protest and the following year I travelled to Australia where the protests followed almost exactly the same sequence, with the Springbok rugby tour followed by stopping the planned cricket tour. A template had been created.'

South Africa would eventually be welcomed back into the rugby fold in 1992 after the end of apartheid. There is a picture of Table Mountain, which provides such a dramatic backdrop to Cape Town, near the President's Room in Twickenham Stadium with a plaque that reads, 'Presented to the Rugby Football Union in renewed rugby friendship to commemorate England's tour to South Africa in 1994.'

Chapter Eight

Dudley Wood and the
'fifty-seven old farts' controversy

When Dudley Wood arrived at Twickenham in 1986 to take up his new role as secretary, he was amazed to discover the RFU telephone number was ex-directory. The previous secretary, Air Commodore Bob Weighill, saw nothing wrong with maintaining this stance and was very clear in his reasoning when questioned by 'new boy' Wood. Weighill told him: 'We would never be able to handle all the calls – we couldn't cope.'

It was symptomatic of the RFU's belief that whatever happened in English rugby was their responsibility and any information they wanted the public to learn would be released through the proper channels. It harked back to the early days of the Union when telegraph messages could be sent to Twickenham addressed to 'Scrummage'. To many, the Union still appeared happiest with mail arriving in a cleft stick, and this ludicrously antiquated system and attitude grated with Wood's philosophy, as he was all about communication. Wood wanted to make the RFU more user-friendly and his first act was to put the Union's number into the telephone book. Having enjoyed a long and successful career with ICI, Wood was used to modern methods of administration and working practice, which put him immediately at odds with the RFU machine that had not been updated for decades and operated on the basis that 'if it ain't broke, don't fix it'. This had been the same maxim that Harold Clark had been dumbfounded to find in place when he took up position as the Union's first clerk of works in 1964. Thankfully for Wood, his staff were not found – on first meeting – lying under coats drinking off the booze they had rifled from the stores.

Wood, ironically, would eventually leave his role after ten years portrayed by some as rugby's King Canute, trying to unsuccessfully hold back the tide of professionalism that engulfed the game in 1995. Significantly, that was the year before Wood departed, yet he had been responsible for dragging the Union out of its stupor, and while his critics will always focus on how he dealt – or didn't deal – with professionalism, the man himself believes he was a Twickenham reformer. 'When I arrived it was at a time of great change at the RFU and we realised we couldn't carry on the way we had been. Certainly on the committee there was a group that didn't want any change at all and I tell the joke that having become secretary I met the longest-serving committee man and I said to him, "You must have seen a lot of changes in your time," and his response was, "Yes, and I voted against all of them!" There were some like that who didn't want any kind of modernisation but it had to come.'

Wood had served the Union as chairman of the important amateur status committee, which decided if players had by their actions (sneaking off for a rugby league trial etc.) lost the right to play rugby union. Given the importance of that committee it would be fair to assume he was up to speed with the workings of Twickenham and the RFU, but you would be wrong. Wood said, 'When I was appointed as secretary of the RFU, I had never even been to the Union's offices at Twickenham because committee meetings took place at the East India Club in St James's Square or the full committee in the Hilton Hotel. Therefore, it was quite a shock to turn up at Twickenham as the new secretary and to see how they operated and that nothing had really changed over the years. Dear old Bob Weighill – lovely man – hadn't changed anything and the RFU was still ex-directory in 1986. I did ask Bob, "Why are we ex-directory?" and he explained that it would produce too many enquiries for the staff! People had to write to the RFU if they wanted to get in contact and while the committee knew the telephone number, it was kept secret from everyone else.

'I didn't consult the committee about making the RFU telephone number public, I just put a new switchboard in and, of course, we did get a lot of calls. Communication was something I was very keen to improve and every letter we received – unless they were rude – had a personal reply either from myself or, if it was a technical question, I would farm it out to Don Rutherford (technical director of the RFU). I said that every letter had to receive a reply and that is what happened. At that point communications involving the RFU and the world at large were almost nonexistent and so we set up the first press conferences where we could deal with issues that were either raised in questions or we felt needed to be discussed. I realised that it was possible to suggest things that the press might write about by putting them on the agenda, which suited my brief. It all worked quite well and I had a lot of support from [future RFU president] Sir Peter Yarranton. Another move that we made was to open the ground earlier so that the public could make a day of being at Twickenham. Previously, the gates didn't open until 12 noon and I got it to 11 a.m. and wanted to get it to 10 a.m. but that didn't happen. I felt we weren't, as an organisation, friendly enough to the public and we did change a lot of things and people went along with it.

'Another interesting aspect that I noted was that ticket applications were still noted down in a large ledger by hand and it really was quite old-fashioned. I am not criticising the situation, it was just a case of not seeing the necessity to bring it all up to date. I could see very quickly there was an awful lot to be done.'

Wood had spent more than thirty years with ICI but was open to a new career because of the travelling involved to get from his home close to Saffron Walden to his work near Blackburn. A former number-eight who played in the Varsity Match for Oxford at Twickenham, Wood had also

King George V, the most avid of Royal rugby fans, is seen here shaking hands with players before an inter-services match at Twickenham. © *PA/PA Archive/Press Association Images*

Twickenham in the 1930s. The 'look' featured stands on three sides and the great expanse of the South Terrace that would become such a problem as the years, and all those fans, took their toll on the structure. © *Popperfoto/Getty Images*

The home of
English rugby
was a focal point
for protests and
demonstrations th
dogged the 1969–
Springbok tour.
© S&G/S&G and Barra
EMPICS Sport

Peter Hain, the man
who masterminded the
1969–70 protests and
who had no idea that
fellow campaigners had
broken into Twickenham
and burnt a Swastika on
the centre of the pitch.
© Popperfoto/Getty Images

Streaker
Michael
O'Brien, who
was fined £10
for his 1974
performance.
This was
followed some
years later by
Erica Roe's
famous topless
run on to the
Twickenham
pitch.
© Getty Images

Brian Moore, the England hooker, takes on the All Blacks and opposite number Sean Fitzpatrick in particular. © *Eye Ubiquitous/Alamy*

A legend is born; Chris Oti, the England winger, with captain Will Carling at his side as 'Swing Low, Sweet Chariot' greets his hat-trick against Ireland. © *Bob Thomas/Getty Images*

John Clark, the Clerk of Works, and his team clear snow from the pitch covers with the new North Stand in the background

© *Murray Sanders/ Associated News/REX*

Dudley Wood, the former RFU Secretary, who could not believe the Union was ex-directory when he started and who became a central figure as the sport became professional. © *Getty Images*

The final piece of the jigsaw: plans for the new South Stand development held by (from left to right) Richard Knight, stadium director, Terry Ward, architect, Francis Baron, former RFU CEO and Derek Morgan, RFU President (2008–9). © *Getty Images*

top: The famous Twickenham hanging room baths, big enough for two players to use. There are still two in both the home and away changing rooms today.
© *Colorsport/REX*

above: The England changing room: the new look 'space age' version that is light years away from the basic space the players were previously accustomed to.
© *David Rogers – RFU/Getty Images*

Keeping the Twickenham pitch in pristine condition; groundsman Keith Kent hard at work on his beloved green carpet. © *Getty Images*

Princess Diana with Princes William and Harry, on her surprise visit to watch an English training session at Twickenham, accompanied by Colin Herridge in the blue and white tracksuit top. © *Glenn Harvey/REX*

Will Carling introduces Her Majesty the Queen to Dean Richards, the England No.8, who produces an impressive bow.

© *Popperfoto/Getty Images*

Rugby mad Prince Harry with his brother Prince William and sister-in-law Kate, finding it more fun to watch a match amongst the crowd than in the Royal Box. © *Andrew Fosker/REX*

The ultimate rugby prize: Captain Martin Johnson lifts the Rugby World Cup after England defeated Australia in the 2003 final in Sydney. © *AFP/Getty Images*

Putting on a show for 82,000 fans at Twickenham. The England versus Wales game, featuring large national flags on the pitch and pyrotechnics off it. *© Getty Images*

Dylan Hartley and Tom Wood raise the Premiership trophy after Northampton's 2014 triumph over Saracens with a packed Twickenham providing the perfect backdrop. *© Getty Images*

appeared at the stadium in club matches against Harlequins during his time with Bedford and Rosslyn Park, and recalls the changing rooms featuring 'those big old baths' and remembers it as 'a funny old place'. He never envisaged coming back in a professional capacity but, having travelled the world with ICI, the weekly trek up to Lancashire meant he was more than interested when the RFU advertised for a new secretary to replace the retiring Weighill.

'When I applied for the job it was a last-minute affair and I was working near Blackburn for ICI and was travelling up every Sunday night and coming back on the Friday night. I did that for a few years and we were successfully turning around a business. I was driving down the A1 one Friday night thinking, I am going to kill myself in an accident if I keep on doing this, and I knew that the RFU job was coming up as Bob Weighill, the secretary, was retiring. I put in an application, was short-listed and interviewed a number of times before being offered the job. I didn't anticipate that happening!

'I was chairing the amateur status committee, having not been on the committee very long, and so I spoke to a board member who said, "Let me talk to John Harvey-Jones," who was the chairman of ICI at that point. Harvey-Jones rang me and said he had learned that I had been offered the job at Twickenham and asked if I wanted to take it. I said, "I don't know," and he said it would be a good job for an ICI man to do and if I wanted to take it, they would make me redundant with a full package, and so I didn't have to decide. I accepted the job as secretary of the RFU and it was announced to the press. Unfortunately, the only person I hadn't told was my wife, and David Hands, *The Times* rugby correspondent, rang my home and asked her, "What do you think of your husband's new job?" to which she replied, "What new job?" He realised he was on tricky ground and so quickly asked, "Will you be moving to Twickenham?" and she replied, "I am not moving anywhere." I had been at ICI for thirty years and thoroughly enjoyed my time and she didn't think I would ever leave.'

Wood had a very inauspicious start, having to postpone his first international as secretary in January 1987 due to heavy snow that meant Scotland could not travel down to Twickenham. 'The Scots rang and said that half their players were in the Borders and only a helicopter would be able to get them out and they would never have been down on the Wednesday. Twickenham station was closed due to the snow and I realised that if we were going to postpone it we had to do it on the Wednesday to give people time. I got hold of the president and he went along with the decision – he wasn't very happy – and we agreed a new date in April with Scotland and announced the postponement and the new date on the Wednesday. I thought that was fine until the BBC rang me and went ballistic. They said, "You didn't consult us," and I said it was nothing to do with them and that we decide when to play and they cover it. They were furious and it emerged – I didn't realise – that we had chosen the same date as the Grand National at Aintree. It was resolved by the Grand National being shown on BBC1 and the England versus Scotland match on BBC2. Not for the last time the BBC were very angry with me.

'I had to feel my way carefully because the committee

were a bit wary of this new chap who had come in. I had to gain their confidence to be able to do things the way I wanted them done.'

Wood's tenure coincided with seismic changes to world rugby, with the first World Cup being staged in New Zealand in 1987 and England then hosting – with the help of the other Five Nations teams – the 1991 tournament. It was the arrival of the World Cup that forced the RFU, as we have seen, to instigate the rebuilding of the North Stand and Wood was to play a significant role in shaping the new horseshoe-shaped stadium while wrestling with the increasingly loud calls for the game to go 'open'. The 1991 World Cup saw the England players attempt to cash in on their increased profile, and men like outspoken hooker Brian Moore and captain Will Carling would be in the vanguard, trying to get the RFU to soften its stance on amateurism. Wood has always been painted as the main obstacle to any change, and he makes no excuses for resisting calls for an open game until the International Rugby Board stunned the sport by announcing the game had become professional in August 1995, in the wake of the World Cup in South Africa.

Wood to this day believes his stance was correct, arguing that the IRB's decision to suddenly announce fundamental change was preferable to allowing the news to leak out. 'I was actually delighted the game went open in 1995. You couldn't go on like it had been and I was always seen as the person battling against the move to a professional game, but you couldn't give a hint that this was going to come about because people would have taken over. When the

IRB announced it was now open, I was criticised for not preparing the way, but you couldn't prepare the way.'

The RFU opted to instigate a one-year moratorium, which appeared to confirm the view that they hoped the whole dreadful idea of a professional game would go away. It didn't. By the time the RFU decided to follow the lead of other Unions and sign up their top players, they discovered England's top clubs, led by wealthy backers such as Nigel Wray (Saracens), Sir John Hall (Newcastle) and Keith Barwell (Northampton), had already got the big names to sign contracts. Instead of controlling the sport, the RFU now found the clubs owned the best players; it signalled the start of a long internecine war that did no one any good. The clubs kept professional rugby going but a collective £150m was spent before peace finally broke out, with agreed funding from the RFU and the clubs releasing their England players for longer periods of national duty. The two sides now live together, but tensions remain.

Wood accepts that the moratorium was a mistake and said, 'I don't think the moratorium worked and it wasn't a good idea. I was offered another year as secretary and I declined and I got out when I could because the pressure really was building following the decision to go open.'

Wood's time as secretary is important in the history of Twickenham and will always be associated with one incident that has become so well known it is even featured in the World Rugby Museum in the stadium. It revolves around an off-camera comment by England captain Will Carling which, unbeknown to him, was recorded by the microphone being used for the television interview. In what he thought was an off-the-record comment, Carling called the RFU Committee 'fifty-seven old farts' in 1995 as the tensions between the players and the Union were reaching breaking point, and it was a comment that would see him stripped, if only briefly, of the captaincy. What many including Carling do not know is that, far from being the man who wanted Carling to lose the captaincy, Wood maintains that he actually asked Dennis Easby, the RFU president, *not* to take such action.

There is no doubt that Wood was the main target for player anger at that time but the man himself pleads innocence to this particular charge. 'Will Carling actually missed me with that comment because I wasn't a member of the committee! It has lived on ever since that happened when his comment was caught off camera and I don't think Will Carling meant it to be recorded. There was an executive committee meeting called immediately after it happened and the president wanted to strip him of the captaincy and there were about eight of us in the meeting. It was agreed that would happen and then the president turned to me and asked what I thought. I said it would be a mistake to sack him – but I was overruled. They did take the captaincy away and Will Carling has always held that against me when, in fact, I was against it, along with Bill Bishop from Cornwall. All hell broke loose because Carling was very popular in the country. Brian Moore wrote in his autobiography and suggested I was behind it and I wrote to him and put it right. It's all history now and it was a difficult period for the game.' Carling subsequently issued a statement in which he apologised unreservedly for any offence caused by his comment.

For his own part, Easby was given full and unequivocal backing by the RFU for his conduct throughout the sacking and subsequent reinstatement of Carling as captain.

Brian Moore, the former England hooker, has a clear memory of the Carling sacking; it epitomised, for him, the massive divide between the players, who wanted to start moving towards professionalism, and Wood, seen as the greatest obstacle in their path to the Promised Land. 'When they sacked Will Carling it was just six weeks away from the 1995 World Cup in South Africa. I was one of the players who was offered the captaincy and it was something I had always wanted to do – lead my country. But I told the RFU there was absolutely no way I was taking over from Will and they got the same message from everyone else in the squad. I have some wonderful memories of playing for England at Twickenham and we were a good side, winning the Grand Slam in 1991, '92 and '95. Incredibly, when we won the Slam in 1991, the first announcement over the PA system was to inform the supporters that Grand Slam merchandise was available in the Twickenham shop. They congratulated the team after that had been broadcast!'

With the rest of the national team refusing to take up the captaincy after he had been sacked, it was clear the players were starting to flex their muscles. Carling was quickly reinstated and would lead the England team at the 1995 World Cup shortly after the 'old farts' incident. With the game going open in August that year, Wood knew it was time to go. The pressure to embrace sponsors and bow to their money-making ways was now a financial imperative, and Wood's previous attitude to the changing face of the game had delayed some of the innovations that would become commonplace. 'The committee were happy to go along with the development of the hospitality side of the stadium. I remember during the amateur days, Mike Coley [RFU marketing director] came to me saying he could get £100,000 for advertising on the post pads and I said, "No, thanks." But times change and now we have advertising on the pitch.'

It would be harsh to paint Wood as a man who spent his time saying 'No' to attempts to boost the coffers of the Union, and he was responsible for helping improve the success of the only Twickenham shop that operated at the ground when he came into the job. A chance meeting over lunch provided Wood with the opportunity to tap into real expertise when it came to maximising the shop's potential. 'When I started we had one shop in the southeast corner of the ground and I was at a lunch at Twickenham and sitting next to me was Sir Ian MacLaurin, the chairman of Tesco. He said that he understood we had a shop and that he would like to see it. I took him down there and he said, "You can do better than this. Shall I send a couple of people down?" He sent a retired director and another chap and they reorganised the shop and suggested we had more outlets. They made it self-service and now, of course, the various Twickenham shops do amazing business on match days and are also online. It all started with the chairman of Tesco!'

Wood initially dealt with the De La Rue company, famous for printing banknotes, who were contracted to deliver the all-important match tickets to Twickenham. However, Wood decided to take the printing in-house, 'which was a great help and it meant we could put the names of the clubs and individuals who were being sent them on the ticket.' Sorting out the ticketing of Twickenham was critical, particularly as there had been 'near misses' when the ground still had terraces. 'I remember talking to Micky Steele-Bodger [former RFU president and IRB chairman] who said there could have been as many as 100,000 fans in the ground for one of the matches during the time when we had terraces. I used to stand on the South Terrace and it was really packed.' With the ground now an all-seater, Wood was spared the job which previous secretaries had undertaken – most notably the longest serving, Sydney F. Coopper – that of helping move spectators from the notorious South Terrace to areas where there was less congestion, by yelling through a large megaphone while standing on a ringside bench.

One of the other major successes Wood was responsible for achieving at Twickenham involved creating areas for wheelchair users and their carers to watch international matches. It is a sad fact that so many major stadia still fail to adequately cater for disabled fans, and rugby has been fortunate to have the Wooden Spoon Society to help raise funds. Wood had been dismayed to discover Twickenham Stadium's facilities for the disabled were nothing to boast about. 'I was concerned that accesses for wheelchair supporters when I arrived were virtually nonexistent. There were barely half a dozen wheelchair users and they were out in the rain with people walking in front of them during the match. It was appalling and so we moved them to a higher level and now we can offer over six hundred places to wheelchair fans and their carers. They come free of charge and have their own bar and elevator and I am very proud of what we built and I was honoured to receive a plaque marking what we had done. The Wooden Spoon charity contributed to the facilities we now offer.' In 2015 the RFU decided to end free tickets for disabled fans opting to bring in a £41 per person charge on the basis of equality with an expected £150,000 to be raised from home games and to boost charity coffers. However, carers and friends accompanying disabled fans still get in for nothing.

While Wood was in charge of Twickenham very few things avoided his influence, but he was kept completely in the dark about a special royal visit. Not surprisingly, Wood was less than pleased to discover it had taken place, but he wasn't alone in being caught off guard. John Clark, the clerk of works, was busy in the England dressing room while the players took part in what he believed was just another regular training workout on the pitch in 1995. The changing room door suddenly opened and in came one of his staff with the news that Princess Diana, the most famous woman in the world, was standing on the side of the pitch with her sons, Princes William and Harry. Not surprisingly, Clark, whose role included calling at Buckingham Palace to collect the Royal Standard in the build-up to the normally carefully choreographed royal visits, headed out to the pitch believing he was the victim of a wind-up. But there she was. Clark remembers chatting with a very relaxed mother watching her sons playing, and said: 'Princess Diana was standing by the tunnel and I asked her if she was coming to the match on Saturday. She said, "No, we have to go to Wales – two hours there, two hours at the match and two hours back." Clark had to break off his conversation to help his men disperse a group of paparazzi who had managed to gain entrance to the North Stand with their long-lens cameras and were busily snapping the shots that would appear in the next day's tabloid papers.

The surprise visit to training was arranged by England captain Will Carling, whose close friendship with the princess would keep him in the tabloid headlines for months. Evidently, Diana had asked if she could watch training and bring the two sports-mad princes along as well, and Carling turned to his friend Colin Herridge, then acting as team manager Jack Rowell's media advisor, to handle the intricate problems of arranging for Diana and her sons to be present at what was supposed to be a closed England session. Herridge was understandably concerned about the visit as he was sworn to secrecy, which meant keeping Dudley Wood and the RFU president Dennis Easby in the dark. Normally, the great and the good and those who were just desperate to be involved in anything remotely to do with royalty would have jostled for position in an official RFU greeting line, but this was no ordinary visit, hence the need for total secrecy. Herridge remembered: 'Princess Diana's visit came about through her friendship with Will Carling, who rang me up one day and told me the princess was going to come to Twickenham with the two princes, William and Harry, to watch England train on a weekend and it had to be hush-hush and would I look after her. They arrived on the east side of the stadium in a car with their detective and I took them around to where we were all standing with Jack Rowell, the England manager, and Tony Hallett.

'I talked to her because Will and the players were out on the pitch and asked what she and the princes liked watching on TV and they said *Baywatch*. She then said, "What do we call it?" and they said "Crutchwatch!" I took everyone into the changing rooms to meet the players and arranged for the princes to get a bag of kit each and they kicked a few balls around on the pitch. Then, on the Monday, I got a rocket from Dudley Wood, the secretary, for not telling him about the royal visit. I was sworn to secrecy and photographers did follow her to the stadium and managed to get into the North Stand until John Clark and his staff cleared them away. There were some great photographs of Princess Diana and the princes laughing on the pitch and it was very surreal watching the England team training with the two princes desperate to get out onto the pitch. She sent me a lovely note after the visit saying they had really enjoyed the occasion.'

Other visits to Twickenham by the royals followed the expected protocol, except for another request from Diana. This time, far from being kept in the dark, Wood was the man earmarked for the difficult assignment. He weighed up the pros and cons of the proposal. 'I got a telephone call and was told that Princess Diana wanted to come to a game with her sons at Twickenham anonymously and would I look after her. I had retired as secretary by then and I said no, because I just knew something would blow up the day before and I would be under pressure.' Wood had been much happier when, as secretary, his role involved officially greeting the Princess Royal, the enthusiastic patron of the Scottish RFU. Police would give a warning when Princess Anne was about to drive up in her official car, which had special resonance one year as she had recently been fined for speeding. 'I remember

Princess Anne coming to an England versus Scotland match in her role as patron of the SRU and the police used to ring through and tell us that the royal party would be at the main gate in five minutes, and so I would head down to greet her with the president. The week before Princess Anne had been fined for speeding on the M4, she was driving when the car arrived at Twickenham and I said, "Lovely to see you, Ma'am, I hope you kept to the speed limit," and she replied, "Don't you start!" She was a very popular visitor to Twickenham and her support of Scottish rugby is remarkable.'

The Queen came to Twickenham twice during Wood's time at the helm of the RFU, once for the Rugby World Cup final and the other occasion was the opening of the new East Stand. While the monarch was more likely to be seen at race meetings rather than rugby matches, the same could not be said for George V, the most regular royal spotted at Twickenham. George V is one of five monarchs to have reigned during the time Twickenham has been the home of English rugby and special measures were taken to ensure he enjoyed every visit. The RFU installed a window at the front of the Royal Box which could be wound up – like a car window – whenever rain or wind threatened to cause discomfort for those inside. There was also a hot-water pipe which ran near the feet of the royals, who sat on special red wicker chairs. One of the technical problems that organisers had when the King was due surrounded the band, which was standing facing the Royal Box. Of course, the bandmaster was looking at his men, not the Royal Box, and wouldn't know when to start the national anthem on the King's arrival. This conundrum was solved by the installation of a red light that a Union official turned on as the King entered the box and which could be seen by the band-master. Royal family members now attend England matches without any fanfare and are happy to be well-known faces in the crowd, with Prince Harry a regular at Twickenham while his cousin Zara Phillips, daughter of Princess Anne, uniquely brought the royal family and rugby together when she married Mike Tindall in 2011, just before the England centre headed to New Zealand as part of the England World Cup squad. The pair had first met in the aftermath of England's historic 2003 World Cup triumph in Sydney, when Prince Harry had also joined the celebration party.

Twickenham Stadium's relationship with the royal family is recorded in a special 24-photograph history displayed in frames on a wall in the Members' Lounge. The first photograph shows George V attending the Royal Navy vs Army match in 1920, accompanied by the Prince of Wales. George V also watched the England vs Wales (1923), England vs France (1926) and England vs Scotland (1928) matches, and was also a frequent visitor when Harlequins staged their club matches.

In 1929 the Duke of York, who would later be crowned George VI, was the principal guest for the England match with Ireland, while the future Edward VIII, then the Prince of Wales, met the teams on the pitch before the match. The Varsity Match of 1937 had George VI in attendance and he came back a year later for the England vs Scotland encounter. After the Second World War, it was the Duke of Edinburgh who assumed the role of frequent royal presence at Twickenham, meeting the players who took part in the Royal Navy vs RAF match in 1948; he would return for England vs Wales (1949), England vs South Africa (1952) and Royal Navy vs Army (1953). The Queen's first visit after her coronation came in 1955 when she brought a young Prince Charles along with the Duke of Edinburgh to watch the Royal Navy vs Army game. There have been sporadic visits since then, with the Queen present for England vs Scotland (1965), England vs New Zealand (1967), England vs President's Overseas XV (1971), Oxford vs Cambridge (1972) and the 1991 World Cup final. The Queen also opened the East Stand in 1994, while the Duke of Edinburgh did the duties with the West Stand in 1995. Princess Anne had opened the North Stand in 1991. The Queen's visits to Twickenham meant the RFU had to hire a red carpet to ensure a royal welcome, and this came under John Clark's list of responsibilities, with Her Majesty having sole use of the committee ladies' toilet during her visit. 'There was a set of stairs leading up from a milling-around area near the changing rooms up to the committee room upstairs with a toilet at the top which was the Queen's toilet. It was used by the committee's ladies but it was out of bounds when Her Majesty attended a match. I don't know what the committee ladies had to do then!'

After Wood had decided to leave his role, Twickenham came under the direction of new secretary Tony Hallett, but there were forces battling for control of the soul of the sport and he would last just over two years, after having been such a key personality, along with Wood, in creating the modern Twickenham Stadium. Now, the RFU was embracing a new professional world, and Twickenham would be central to the Union generating annual turnover of more than £150m by 2014.

Chapter Nine

The changing Twickenham
changing rooms

Brian Moore, according to legend and information supplied to visitors on guided trips around the stadium in the mid-1990s, was responsible for a dark stain on the England dressing room wall after losing the 1991 Rugby World Cup final to Australia. 'Not true,' said Moore, who won sixty-four caps as a combative and erudite hooker and is now a successful author and member of the media. 'That is a complete fabrication.' Access to the England dressing room has always been restricted, which used to give the room an air of mystery and allowed myths like Moore's stain to be created. Other sports, most notably the National Football

League and Major League Baseball in North America, allow television cameras and the media to swarm into the changing rooms after matches, and there is a more relaxed attitude in European rugby. Those sporting bodies recognise they are operating in a market place and the players are a commodity that need to be made available to the fans and those who act as a conduit between the two.

That has never been the RFU's stance; even in this professional era, access to the players is carefully controlled and the changing rooms are still off limits. For decades the England changing room and the one for the away team constituted the only areas where players could put on their kit in the stadium. Since the development of the West Stand in the middle of the 1990s there have been six changing rooms and enhanced facilities for the match officials, who used to operate out of one small referee's room. Twickenham's earliest changing rooms featured a bench for players to sit on running along the walls and hooks where clothes could be hung up. In 1931 the RFU installed the now famous cast-iron baths produced by Allied Ironfounders for players to use in both the home and away areas. There were half a dozen in each changing room and these were half-filled with cold water and then the hot was added just before the final whistle by the changing-room attendant.

Twickenham Stadium was not alone in offering rudimentary facilities for the players, as for much of the amateur era the attitude of the governing bodies who ran the sport and picked the national teams was that a player was lucky to have the opportunity to represent his country and didn't need to be pampered. Players, before the era of sponsored kit, would be asked to bring their own boots, shorts and socks and also had to supply their own training jersey – even for international squad sessions.

Bill Beaumont, the RFU chairman, led England out to Grand Slam glory in 1980 from Twickenham changing rooms that would look exactly the same when Will Carling sprayed champagne to toast England's 1991 Slam triumph. Beaumont said, 'The first time I came to Twickenham was to see England versus Ireland when Tony O'Reilly was recalled to the wing for Ireland in 1970. I never thought I would ever play there and so when I came back in December 1974 for an England trial I was thinking, well, if nothing else, at least I have played there.

'The strongest memory of Twickenham at that time was the big baths and the beautifully polished wooden floor. Before the kick-off, the baths would be half-full of cold water and they would top them up with hot at the end of the game. There were just two shower heads in the corner, while your England jersey was hung on a hook. Starting on the left-hand side, the shirt numbers went from one to fifteen around the room. You had to bring your own shorts and socks and if you needed a new pair of England socks you had to see Ken, the changing room attendant. You got a new pair when you handed the old ones back. For England training you wore your own kit and I had a jersey I had got on tour in South Africa with Northern Counties from the game with Northern Transvaal. I trained in that at each session, which is in total contrast to the kit the players get now. The England team can change jerseys at half-time if they want.

'The prize thing to get as an England player when I was playing was the purple tracksuit with the red rose and the three adidas stripes down the arms. Woe betide your girlfriend or wife if they put it on anything but a forty-degree wash because everything else would be turned a shade of purple. I didn't get mine until after I had actually played for England in 1975 and I remember travelling to Twickenham with Tony Richards, a wing at Fylde with me who then played at Wasps and went on tour with England in 1972 to South Africa. We got on the train to London for a trial match when we were both in the "Rest" team and we talked about how we would fill our boots with swag – new boots, trainers, tracksuits etc. – and we got nothing! If you were in the Rest team you took navy shorts and your club top while the England team got the real kit. If you ever got taken off at Twickenham from the Rest team by the selectors, you knew that was it. You were never going to feature in the England squad. The England jersey was really heavy and I always used to roll my sleeves up on my jersey to play – these days you would just cut them off to the required length. In a match I would spend the whole of the second half rolling up those sleeves because they would get heavier and heavier as the material got wetter and wetter. The Scottish players used to get one jersey for the season and if they wanted to swap with the opposition then they had to pay for it. You had to really get on well with your Scottish opposite number to get them to swap because it cost guys like Gordon Brown and Alan Tomes money! I still have my purple England tracksuit and it is in a bag some-where at home.'

When John Clark took over as clerk of works in 1982, ensuring the changing room operated properly was just one of his many jobs. The only medical room at that point had been built some years earlier by his father, Harold. John explained: 'I realised in my first or second game at Twickenham as clerk of works that it wasn't my job to actually watch England playing – I had to keep my eyes and ears open for any problems. I knew who had won by the look on the England players' faces when they came back to the changing rooms. In 1982 there was a tunnel leading from the pitch with the public hanging over the walls and then you went into a corridor running the length of the West Stand. There were just home and away dressing rooms along with a cupboard containing laces, studs and pumps for the balls. The dressing rooms had wood-block floors with benches around the walls and pegs to hang clothes. There were the famous baths and the two showers in the corner with a concrete floor and tiles on the wall. In the area outside the dressing rooms – a milling-around bit – my father had built the surgery for Dr Leon Walkden, the RFU doctor. The dressing rooms were virtually identical and the jerseys would have been hung up on the pegs for the players.

'Despite running the Middlesex Sevens with all those teams taking part, there were just two dressing rooms at Twickenham. There are now six, but you can imagine the chaos with half the Sevens teams in one dressing room and the other half in the second one. There was mayhem. The referees had a little room under the stairs on the same level as the dressing rooms. When we started having two county matches on the same day we had to get the timings absolutely spot-on so we could get two teams in and out and then clean the dressing rooms for the next two and so on. It was amazing how we managed it and then when we had six dressing rooms we had four games on the same day, which meant finding room for eight teams!'

One feature of the Twickenham changing rooms before the West Stand was rebuilt concerned a set of stairs that led down from the RFU Committee area (with bar) which had a small gate to stop 'unwanted' guests from going up to where the great and the good of the game were enjoying a pre-match drink. Of course, the gate didn't stop well-oiled committee grandees from heading down to the changing rooms before kick-off to deliver what they believed would be a well-received 'Have a good game, old boy'. For Moore, this was the most annoying aspect of life as an England player at Twickenham. Moore famously threw his runners-up medal into the Thames, such was his disappointment at losing in the 1991 World Cup final at Twickenham to Australia. His emotions always ran close to the surface, which helped make him an incredible competitor, on and off the pitch. 'Outside the changing rooms was a set of stairs with a latched gate at the bottom which led up to the committee area. It allowed various committee people to come down, drink in hand, and believe they had the right to wish us "good luck" by slurring that out. I complained to Dudley Wood about these people being allowed to interrupt our preparations for a match and, typically, he saw nothing wrong with members of the RFU Committee getting that kind of access. The RFU attitude was that the players were only there for a short period and that they – the committee – were permanent.

After I had used a few words to Micky Steele-Bodger who came down the steps, I was called before Dudley Wood after a complaint had been made. I confirmed what I had said and thankfully that "custom" of wishing the team good luck stopped after that!

'The old changing rooms were fine, with the only significant addition during my time being a scrum machine that allowed us to have a few "hits" before we ran out. I had a lot of fondness for the old changing facilities which I thought had enough room and have now been replaced with individual areas. The old baths remain and there are various medical rooms while we only had the dentist's area, which was used for stitching minor cuts. Getting onto the pitch meant running up a couple of steps and I would always tell myself, "Don't make a prat of yourself and stumble," and the atmosphere in the old stadium was amazing. There was a low wall running around the pitch and Nigel Melville, the England captain fell near it and broke his leg in 1988. You were really close to the crowd; standing on the touchline waiting to throw the ball into the line-out, I could hear individual comments from fans, and the new stadium has lost that intimacy. Only the Millennium Stadium has retained the old feel.'

The state of the changing rooms concerned Clive Woodward when he took over as head coach in 1997 and, as someone who had no problem asking the RFU to fund changes designed to help make the team number one in the world, he got his way. In his book *Winning!* Woodward charts the differences he made to a room that still had the same barren and functional feel as when he used it as an England player in the 1980s. This was despite the fact that it had been rebuilt as part of the West Stand development just a couple of years earlier. He said:

> The players' changing room at Twickenham was as inspiring as a prison cell. Bare, grey breeze block wall, a lone unpolished wooden bench underneath a row of wooden pegs. We at least wanted a coat of paint with some colour. The ground committee with whom I discussed the problem could not understand. 'The changing room is only a few years old. What's wrong with it?' They wouldn't direct any money to the improvements and so, thinking laterally, we came up with the idea of calling the TV show *Real Rooms* and they jumped at the chance to make-over our changing room. As a surprise for the players, we kept it a secret until the Wales game of the Five Nations. When they walked in, it was a complete transformation. Fresh paint in vibrant colours, individual cubicles with hand-carved English oak name placards for each player. England imagery 'To be the best' everywhere along with the England Rose and St George Cross.

It seems remarkable that the England head coach had to go cap in hand to a television production company to instigate a new, updated look for the room where the players spent the last crucial hours before the international matches that produced millions of pounds of gate receipts. This was the period just before the RFU employed their first paid chief executive, Francis Baron, who would provide the funding for Woodward's many ground-breaking initiatives that helped deliver the Rugby World Cup in 2003. Woodward was able to keep the dramatic changing-room update secret because England did not train at Twickenham Stadium. He moved the squad's training base to the five-star Pennyhill Park Hotel near Bagshot, which quickly gained a rugby pitch and remains the first-choice base for the national team. It allows the players to travel to Twickenham on match day by coach and spend only forty minutes in traffic. Substantial change is happening at Pennyhill Park, with an indoor training facility being built and the pitch getting the same attention and treatment head groundsman Keith Kent delivers at the stadium.

Woodward's improvements at least moved the changing rooms into the professional rugby era, but the most radical overhaul was instigated by head coach Stuart Lancaster in 2013 and was an integral part of his drive to make the current England players aware of those who had worn the jersey before them. Not surprisingly, it was a costly exercise, and the result was compared by some to the control deck of the starship *Enterprise* from *Star Trek*, including a large disc on the ceiling featuring five of the coach's buzzwords: teamwork, respect, enjoyment, discipline and sportsmanship. 'It looks space-age from the photos but it is not,' insisted Lancaster. 'It's obviously modern but it makes you appreciate the history of England rugby, which is what we wanted. It was a combination of people's ideas. I pulled it together. But Matt Parker [once of British Cycling but now the RFU's head of athletic performance] did a great job in working with the designers. When we got in there we could show the players the history wall, the debut board and also behind each player's changing spot were the names of those who had played in their position before. So you get across the point that you are not just playing for your friends and family but also those who have played previously in your position. The RFU had decided to make a change in the lead-up to the World Cup in 2015. We had various options and configurations. There was a pillar in the changing room and it was going to be in the middle of the room and you wanted to have all the players in your eye-line and so we reconfigured it. It then came down to how it should feel and I had some strong views on it and the ultimate strength is that we are on the same page with the RFU and we ended up with a modern, professional changing room with an old-school feel to it – which is quite hard to achieve. We wanted to have a link with the past. We wanted plaques behind each number, which says you are one of us. The top ten most capped number-eights will be listed in the number-eight area and it makes you feel part of a special club. The corridor has famous moments from England's past, and we have messages we want to get across and the history of England. In the tunnel there is the ability for fans to tweet messages that the players can read and it all adds up. People may not think that little things like that matter but I believe they do. We could have messed about with the away changing room but we wanted to be professional in all of this and give them a good room as well. Those things come back to bite you on the backside anyway!'

So what did Lancaster create for his England players and, to a lesser extent, the opposition? The first striking difference is that the home and away teams now have their own entrances to the changing rooms and that helps to immediately give the England players a clear idea that this is 'their' territory. After walking past the changing rooms for match officials – both male and female areas – and an anti-doping room where players chosen at random from both teams have to provide post-match samples for testing, the players are faced with a wall covered by a large photograph of the England team lined up for the national anthem. They then turn right, which takes them into the tunnel area, and the home changing room is on the left. Through the double doors, you walk along a corridor which has, to its left, a grey, granite-like wall covered in historic moments and scores special to England, and the number of caps won by iconic players from all eras of the sport. This opens up into a large room split in two by a partition which features a huge flat-screen television. This faces into the England changing area, with each player having his own area framed in wood and matched in red-and-white branding. The red cushioned seat is placed in front of each section with the player's name on a plaque, and below this are listed ten players who have played in the position in the past. There are lift-up doors that reveal storage areas and a hook to hang jackets and jerseys from. Above the players is the disc with the core values written along its rim.

Through a short passageway is the management changing area, preceded by the debut board which lists the names of every player who has made his England debut and the year they played. The management do not have individual panelled changing areas but the colour scheme is the same. Before their room is a section for the technical analysts to set up their equipment, with numerous power sockets. Moving back towards the players' changing area, on the right is the England medical team's section, with four padded massage tables and a small kitchen area with a sink and refrigerator. The toilets are off to one side and a short walk takes you into the infamous ice-bath zone. Two large hydro baths stand alongside the remaining two – of the original six – 1931 iron baths that have been re-enamelled and painted white with large silver taps. These get filled with ice for players to lie in after matches, a process designed to limit the damage caused to muscles from heavy hits. There is a new shower section with twelve showers. The room also features four digital clocks in various areas to ensure everyone knows how long it is until kick-off.

As Lancaster pointed out, England have not messed around with the visitors' changing room, which is on the opposite side of the tunnel and, like the England one, is accessed by electronic key. The visitors' area is smaller than England's, featuring eleven showers and two iron baths, but they do not have ice baths. There are also four digital clocks and a management changing facility, plus one massage bed in the medical zone. Significantly, the colour scheme is also England red and white! The tunnel is now much more than just a corridor leading to the pitch and features lighting in the ceiling, which is red and white for England matches but can be changed to reflect the colours of other competitions, such as the Heineken Cup. The tweeted fan messages featured on the tunnel wall are chosen to reflect their words of support, with the best one chosen by captain Chris Robshaw, which earns the sender the chance to meet the players. Just before the partly frosted folding doors, which are opened right up on match days, is an area to the right where television and radio 'flash' interviews take place in six rooms of varying sizes. There are four other changing rooms of more traditional design, featuring pegs and benches and the same colour scheme, along with areas for the ball boys and girls to change, and a fully equipped medical facility and dental practice. Further along the corridor which runs at right angles to the tunnel is an Events Ops room. Here the match-day manager co-ordinates the timing of everything from pre-game programme to the handing in of team sheets.

For Beaumont the money it took to create this new look has been well spent, and he is particularly impressed with the emphasis on reminding the current players that they are merely looking after a jersey that has been worn by so many before them and will be handed on to those who follow. 'The new changing rooms are totally different to my time as a player. It is unbelievable. What they have captured is the history and heritage and what it means to play for England. There is a board with around 1,400 players listed and it doesn't matter if you played for England once or fifty times, your name is up there.'

One of those names belongs to Lawrence Bruno Nero Dallaglio, who would achieve career-defining success for club and country from the 'Home' room under the West Stand. He would also take part in a match that would have been inconceivable before rugby union went open in 1995. A hundred years earlier, in the George Hotel in Huddersfield in 1895, the great divide was created that still means there are two different versions of rugby being played around the world. Three years earlier, Bradford and Leeds rugby clubs had begun to pay players compensation for the work they missed when playing. The RFU was totally against this development and were determined to prevent it. On 29 August in the George Hotel, twenty-one teams set up the Northern Rugby Football Union, which would become, twenty-seven years later, the Rugby League. Similar break-ups would take place within the rugby communities of Australia and New Zealand in 1907. From their league heartland in the north, the professional game saw the RFU as an enemy and took great delight in raiding its ranks for the best talent. Wales, in particular, lost key players because they could make money in league. In England, there were also regular defections, and players put their amateur careers in great danger by playing in matches for league clubs. They would appear in the programme as S.O. Else or A.N. Other. These outings were designed to see if the player could handle the particular demands of the thirteen-man game, and great lengths were taken to keep secret the names of those who stuck their toe in the professional water.

When rugby union went professional in August 1995, there was no longer any reason for secrecy. But instead of a flood of union men heading into league, there was a flow the other way, bringing men like Jason Robinson and Andy Farrell to a sport they had never previously thought about playing. One of the most significant moments in the healing of the rift between league and union came at Twickenham in 1996. Rugby union had been professional for barely a year when the Rugby Football Union sanctioned cross-code matches between Wigan, the greatest team in rugby league, and Bath, who contained a number of England internationals, including Phil de Glanville, Mike Catt, Jon Callard, Steve Ojomoh and Andy Robinson. The idea was to help bring the two codes together now that union had fully embraced the concept of paying its players. The first match took place at Manchester City Football Club's former home at Maine Road (where leaving your car in a side street before the match was a form of Russian roulette). The match, on 8 May, was played under league rules and Wigan destroyed their West Country opponents 82–6. It was a total humliation but at least Bath knew they would be playing under union rules at Twickenham in the return fixture. The league game feaured a double hat-trick of tries from Wigan wing Martin 'Chariots' Offiah, who had been a union player before switching codes and would return to that game.

The return fixture between Wigan and Bath took place at Twickenham two weeks later and the northerners only lost 44–19, which left many to mull over the obvious differ-ence between the teams in term of fitness and ball skills. In between the two games against Bath, Wigan were offered another chance to demonstrate their ability to success-fully cross the great rugby divide by competing in the world-famous RFU Middlesex Sevens competition – they responded by beating a Wasps side led by a young flanker called Lawrence Dallaglio 38–15 in the final. The magni-tude of the task facing Wasps in that final was clear for their squad and everyone else in the stadium to see. You only had to scan down the Wigan team sheet to recognise the gulf in class and professional rugby experience. They had brought a squad that read: Kris Radlinski, Jason Robinson,

Va'aiga Tuigamala, Gary Connolly, Martin Offiah, Henry Paul, Shaun Edwards, Andy Farrell, Rob Smyth and Scott Quinnell.

Dallaglio, one of England's 2003 World Cup-winning heroes and a former captain, first played on the Twickenham pitch as a member of King's House prep school's team and he never imagined the stadium would play such a big part in his sporting life, including this ground-breaking battle with Wigan's rugby league stars. Being a man who likes a challenge, Dallaglio decided that, on leaving the Twickenham changing rooms for the final, he would have to take the game to Wigan. The teams lined up alongside each other in the tunnel, and in those difficult moments before battle commenced, Dallaglio suddenly started ranting and raving about what his fellow Wasps were about to do to Wigan. Looking back, Dallaglio acknowledges this was the action of a desperate man who was facing a final against the best rugby league had to offer at that time, while his Wasps squad was callow in comparison.

That show of defiance by Dallaglio impressed Shaun Edwards, the Wigan playmaker, to such an extent that he started to follow the exploits of this feisty young player and the men in black with the Wasps on the jersey. No one could have imagined that in the years to come, not only would Edwards become a Wasps coach, but he would join the Wales and then British and Irish Lions coaching setups. Dallaglio said: 'Looking at the Wigan side, I knew that this wasn't just a rugby league side about to play at Twickenham; it was one of the greatest league teams ever assembled, containing some of the most outstanding players to ever feature in the game. I remember that the Wasps team in the final was young, naive and inexperienced. Looking down our line there was Andy Gomarsall, Peter Scrivener and Shane Roiser – my mates – and then I turned to the Wigan line and they were led by Shaun Edwards, followed by Henry Paul, Inga Tuigamala, Gary Connolly, Martin Offiah and Jason Robinson. It was unbelievable and my view was, "We haven't got a hope in hell of beating this side even if things go to plan." I started shouting and getting psyched up and we weren't showing them any of the respect they obviously deserved. I am sure the rest of the Wasps boys were thinking that we didn't need to annoy Wigan any more and would I please stop. We actually took an 18–0 lead and then they very casually pulled it back and ran out winners.

'I spoke to Shaun Edwards about that day when he came to coach us and he said he liked Wasps after that match and they became his team in union. When he decided to find a place in union as a coach, Wasps was the first team he thought about and we had some very happy years together winning lots of trophies, with Shaun working very closely with our head coach Warren Gatland, who would go on to become the Wales and British and Irish head coach, winning Grand Slams and a Test series in Australia in 2013.

'Who would have ever predicted that day at Twickenham that from the Wigan line-up Inga Tuigamala and Martin Offiah would be playing union at Wasps, Henry Paul went to Gloucester and played for England, Garry Connolly was going to join Harlequins, Andy Farrell played alongside me for England after joining Saracens and then become England and Lions backs coach, while Jason Robinson joined Sale and scored the only England try when we were both members of the 2003 Rugby World Cup-winning team. It was phenomenal. '

Rugby league brought their showpiece matches to Twickenham – while Wembley was being rebuilt. The opening match of the 2000 Rugby League World Cup between Australia and England was staged at the stadium, and the following year a dour Challenge Cup final in the rain ended with St Helens defeating Bradford Bulls 13–6. There was a much better spectacle in 2006 when St Helens again triumphed in the final, accounting for Huddersfield 42–12 in front of 65,187 fans.

Dallaglio is a west London boy, he supports Chelsea and lives with his family near Richmond Park. His England career covered the most successful period in the team's history with that World Cup triumph in 2003, and the stadium evokes strong memories. 'Growing up in the area and seeing Twickenham change over the years, it has a special place in my heart; Wasps enjoyed lots of success in big finals on the pitch and England had considerable success, turning it into a real fortress. I watched the 1991 Rugby World Cup final at the ground and played across the pitch for my prep school in a festival and scored a try on the West Stand touchline. Twickenham became the second home for Wasps and both the Heineken Cup finals we made – in 2004 and 2007 – were played at the stadium. I believe we played in eleven finals and lost one to Saracens, and the rest were great successes for a club that had a small following but somehow managed to find an army of fans when we had a final at Twickenham.

'As a club, we had a truly amazing journey to Twickenham for that first Heineken Cup final in 2004, winning away in Perpignan in the most hostile atmosphere any of us had experienced, followed by a home victory over Gloucester, an amazing win in Dublin against Munster with a sea of red supporters in the Lansdowne Road stands, and then the success in the final over Toulouse and all of their Galacticos at Twickenham. There was a world-record crowd for a club match in the stadium and in terms of playing budgets it was Dave against Goliath, with Wasps at that stage having around £3m to spend on the squad and Toulouse could afford to shell out £33m. They had a team of fifteen internationals and another seven on the bench and they produced spectacular rugby but we held on and then scored some of our own to clinch a first Heineken Cup. One of the tries was a training-ground move that saw Alex King come back down the short side and Mark Van Gisbergen race away for a fantastic try. We had a ten-year reunion dinner in May 2014 in the Rose Room with the players coming back to Twickenham to mark the achievement of becoming the first English team to win the cup and domestic league title double.'

When he started his England career, the game was still amateur and the RFU was populated by men who were getting increasingly concerned about talk of the sport becoming professional. Dallaglio summed up the attitude among the younger players at that time: 'I first went into the changing rooms in 1993 when I was brought into the England squad and that was when it was still the old West Stand when the whole notion of training at the stadium was unheard of – you probably needed to go through several committees just to be allowed out onto the pitch!' Dallaglio would play his part in ensuring that professional rugby became a success in England, although he still finds it incredible that head coach Clive Woodward failed to get backing to improve the state of the Twickenham changing rooms.

Next to the England changing room is the well-equipped gymnasium with all manner of weights to test a player to the absolute limit. A training 'breakfast club' was created by Dallaglio and like-minded England players who were driven by the desire to become the fittest and most successful team in world rugby in 2003. 'When Clive made the changes to the room he had asked for it to be updated and we all told him the kind of things we wanted and got it funded by the television programme. The transformation of the stadium has been amazing and, as a local resident, I have seen it all taking place. I spent many mornings along with Jason Leonard, Joe Worsley and Will Greenwood in the Twickenham gym, which is just off the dressing rooms, training with Dave Reddin, the England fitness expert. We would meet up at 6 a.m. and get beasted beyond belief in the gym. We did that to get ourselves into the shape to be the best international players we could be. I have seen the new England changing room and it is a fantastic trans-formation. It is an amazingly inspirational place and the inner sanctum looks as good as it ever has. It has become an exciting room. The stadium is very iconic and the noise created by supporters who connect with the players and the atmosphere is as good as anywhere in the world.'

Chapter Ten

A new professional broom, Operation St George and blood on the carpet

While the arrival at Twickenham of Harold Clark instigated fundamental change to the pitch and the working
habits of the men employed to run the stadium, and Dudley
Wood as secretary threw open the RFU office doors and actually
invited the public to communicate with the game's governing
body, the appointment of Francis Baron as the Union's first
chief executive delivered the greatest shock to the system of all.

Baron's reputation as a hard-nosed businessman preceded
him. The media viewed his arrival in 1998 as confirmation
that the RFU, struggling to make money in a newly professional sport, had opted to use this man to 'slash and burn'

the organisation. Twickenham was set for tough times while he was prowling the corridors. It was assumed by outsiders that once Baron had trimmed the workforce and dragged the Union into the modern business world, he would move on to his next basket case. We were wrong. Baron would become the most powerful man in the RFU, hiring the men and women he believed would turn a Union with crippling debts into a financial and playing powerhouse. Clive Woodward's win–loss record as England head coach at the time of Baron's arrival made him vulnerable, and he recounted in his book *Winning!* that there were '130 people in the entire organisation and 34 made redundant'. He called his wife, Jayne, and said, 'I've still got a job but it's been one hell of a morning here.' As he looked back on that period, Woodward's verdict is supportive of Baron, and he wrote: 'Francis Baron's actions during this period, brave and forward-thinking as they were, strengthened my commitment to carry on and complete what I had set out to do.'

That commitment would deliver the 2003 Rugby World Cup, but a year later Woodward, after being knighted, would resign, having failed to get the control he wanted of the elite sport in England, triggering a period of instability that made selling the sport much harder to sponsors. That commercial income was vital to continue the RFU's financial plan and to ensure the vision for Twickenham Stadium could be realised.

Among the thirty-four who were made redundant was Don Rutherford, a man who had spent thirty years with the RFU and was their first professional appointment as technical director in September 1969. He initiated coaching and playing programmes that were emulated by rugby-playing countries across the world; he was made Director of Rugby and built up a nationwide structure, starting with mini-rugby through to the national team, providing a stream of playing talent. But Baron decided he was surplus to requirements, along with former England captain Roger Uttley, who was Woodward's team manager. It was the sacking of these two highly respected and much-liked rugby men that grabbed the headlines and confirmed that Baron was going to be his own man – previous service and reputation would count for little in the battle to save the RFU from financial disaster.

It would be difficult to overstate the need at that time for fundamental change, as the RFU had lost £10.3m in the previous two years. 'When I came to Twickenham in 1998 the RFU was in very serious financial trouble. It was haemorrhaging money and I was tasked with putting in professional management and turning the organisation around,' said Baron, who caused a stir by driving around in an Aston Martin with a personalised number plate. 'It had a major asset in Twickenham Stadium but it was only being used for money-making activities for five times a year and the cost of just maintaining a stadium like Twickenham is about six to eight million pounds in terms of depreciation, maintenance, staffing and security. If it's not generating revenue then it's a millstone around your neck. It was clear to me that the major asset on the balance sheet was costing us money, not making it.'

This was the kind of straight talking that immediately set Baron on a collision course with some of the amateur rugby men who populated the many RFU committees he would lock horns with, seemingly on a daily basis. Having invited the bull into the china shop, there was always going to be damage and, not surprisingly, there were those in the Union who wanted the beast dealt with – and quickly. It was the start of what turned into a long-running and, at times, very acrimonious battle for power within the corridors of Twickenham. Despite Woodward initiating a period of unprecedented success on the pitch for England, culminating in the number-one ranking and victory at the 2003 Rugby World Cup in Australia, off the pitch it was a question of whether Baron could fight off the factions who wanted to control a Union that was now actually making money.

'I joined just after the professional era in rugby had started and the place was in chaos with an amateur organisation trying to move into a professional era on and off the pitch,' he explained. 'The amateur administrators were well intentioned but the place was in a total mess and Cliff Brittle, who had become chairman of the RFU, was fighting the professional clubs and then lost the election in 1998 and Brian Baister took over as chairman. Brian was instrumental in persuading me to take up the reins as the first CEO. Previously, men like Dudley Wood and Tony Hallett had the title of "Secretary of the RFU" and I arrived to find the RFU dominated by fifty-seven committees trying to run the organisation. Committees are not the best form of professional management and tend to be a way of not making decisions. They gave me a clear remit to restructure the RFU and put in professional management to financially turn things around. That was fine initially, but when the change started to happen, you had to stop the committee members trying to take back powers again. You ended up with a non-stop battle to keep the organisation managed professionally while keeping the amateurs motivated because they are vital to the grassroots of the game. However, you have to stop them believing that through a sixty-strong council they can manage a professional operation because they cannot.'

Baron had been given a specific brief when handed the job and, with the Union's balance sheets not adding up, action had to be taken immediately, despite the growing disquiet from the various committees whose existence was questioned by the chief executive. He wanted a slimmer, more focused operation, albeit still involving the amateurs, who remained absolutely convinced that the sport was being hijacked by the English professional clubs, who now owned the top players. Many eyed Baron as an unnecessary and costly addition, a man who did not understand the ethos of the sport – a spurious argument that would continue to do the rounds for years to come.

Baron had little time for committee niceties; he had a Union to save. 'It was important to have a clear remit in my contract to allow me to turn things around and when I announced the redundancies – no one likes doing that – there were a whole section of council members who got very unhappy. We had just had two years of heavy loss-making and had lost £10m in that period before I joined on a turnover of over of only £28m. We had bank borrowings of £38m as a result of the West Stand development and the banks were on the point of calling in those loans because we were in breach of the covenants in the loan agreements. Fairly dramatic action had to be taken pretty swiftly and so I took the necessary decisions against the wishes of a considerable number of RFU Council members who didn't understand how dire the situation was at that moment. I believe we were about six months away from having serious problems with NatWest, who were our bankers. It took a year before I felt things were moving in the right direction and in the second year we were in profit and they grew every year, with the balance sheet looking better, and we brought professional management in, including Nick Eastwood [financial] and Paul Vaughan [commercial].'

Under Baron's direction, the RFU created subsidiary and joint-venture businesses, including Twickenham Experience Ltd, who have the rights to all hospitality within Twickenham Stadium; England Rugby Travel, who sell packages worldwide; the London Marriott Hotel, Twickenham; and the Virgin Active Classic Health Club. Implementing these plans meant assembling like-minded professionals; at the same time, Baron started to deal with the committee structure that had been such a vital part of the Union in the years leading up to the advent of professional rugby in 1995. Looking back at this time of the stadium's life, Baron has a clear memory of the ire brought down upon him by Union members who seemed to view the CEO's plans as an attempt to emasculate them and grab power for himself. Groups of disgruntled RFU members found in Baron a common 'enemy', and a small number plotted to rid themselves of someone they saw as an unwanted intruder who was threatening the basic fabric of the Union.

Baron has no regrets about the manner of his tenure and insists it was strong medicine that had to be administered or the patient would not have recovered. 'I managed to get rid of most of the committees and we went from fifty-seven to four standing committees and it was achieved in a short period of time. I was in the job for twelve years and over that period the RFU Council did come round, grudgingly at times, to what I was proposing for the RFU and

Twickenham, but there was always a small group of difficult people. Overall, council tends to come to the right decision, if by a slightly circuitous path. I had to get Twickenham into a position where it was generating revenue not just on five occasions a year – we needed it to be making money 365 days a year. The key part of the eight-year plan I put in place in 2001 was to get back control of our hospitality operations, which under the amateur era were outsourced to companies who were making the money, not the RFU, and so we set up Twickenham Experience to create our own hospitality company and received £14m up front from our partners and it was a good deal. Conferences and exhibitions was an area we clearly needed to get into and the stadium didn't have the facilities to compete in that market, which made redeveloping the southern end absolutely key. At the south end you could have a hotel, a major retail presence and a health and leisure centre, all of which could be open all year round. The biggest battle with the local authority was to get agreement to hold concerts at Twickenham Stadium, which can make you a profit of a million pounds from each one. That all took a long time to get the relevant permission because we had to go to appeal for concerts – all of these elements were needed to ensure the stadium was earning its keep and now all of those areas are producing good revenue.

'Of course, the Rugby World Cup victory in 2003 did produce a dividend that is probably still with us in some small way. The feel-good factor remained even after Clive Woodward left in 2004 and, while the results weren't as good on the pitch, we were still able to do good deals with sponsors, broadcasters and partners in the South Stand development.

Sponsors tend to take a longer view than rugby media, who concentrate on the most recent results, and you cannot run a business on the back of the last win or loss. You need a clear long-term plan to deliver value to key stakeholders.'

As we will see, Baron managed to sidestep at least two serious attempts to oust him from the CEO's post, and his years at Twickenham have not been unduly clouded by the plotters and the in-fighting. 'I first went to Twickenham when I was at Cambridge University and came up for the Varsity Match in the old stadium with the rather crude bar and hospitality facilities that were attached to the old West Stand. Twickenham now has a complete bowl and the stadium generates serious business with a really nice front door provided by the South Stand. I think it is one of the most impressive stadiums in the world when you walk up from Twickenham station and, while the bowl may not be as dramatic as other stadia, we have added a real signature to the South Stand with the development.

'Every time I visit Twickenham Stadium I feel proud of a job well done and I think it is one of the best in the world. There are very few stadia in the world with the range of facilities it offers and it will be constantly updated as the maintenance bill alone is £3m a year. The RFU is spending more than £70m on a programme of refurbishment prior to the 2015 Rugby World Cup and they have to keep generating profits to justify the investment. If you don't keep doing that then, very quickly, things can start looking tatty. That is what happened in the 1960s; however, the stadium is in place and should generate substantial revenue for the whole game for years to come.'

If forces within the RFU acting against Baron had got

their way, the former CEO would not have been allowed to see the South Stand complex come to life or the business become such a major success. The arrival of professional rugby in 1995 saw the Rugby Football Union take the ridiculously negative step of instigating a moratorium – effectively waiting a year to see if this 'professional thing' went away. Of course it didn't, and by the time the RFU gears were dusted down, oiled and asked to swing slowly into action, England's top players had all been signed up by the leading clubs, not the Union. Power was now with the club owners, who would collectively put around £150m into setting up a truly professional sport in England.

Symptomatic of the RFU's slow response was the realisation that they needed to appoint a chief executive to run the Union. As we have charted, this didn't happen until three years later. The RFU had built a new horseshoe-shaped Twickenham, but who was going to play on the pitch? Patently, the committee-led Union could handle major building projects to secure the future of the national stadium, but they were ill-equipped to deliver a professional game without the addition of seasoned professional businessmen. That is why they appointed Francis Baron. As we have seen, what Baron found was a financial basket case and he immediately sacked more than thirty people to cut the deficit. This put him at odds with the RFU Council, which included a group of men who had lived and breathed the amateur game and believed the grass roots of the sport would die unless someone regained control of rugby from individuals who they saw as the moneymen.

The emergence of men such as Cliff Brittle, Graeme

Cattermole, Brian Baister and Martyn Thomas drew some interest as they each in turn assumed the chairmanship of the RFU, but they were hardly household names. None prevented the in-fighting and name-calling that followed the game going professional in 1995 (which, to an extent, still flares up today), which became the most numbingly boring internecine war ever staged. Egos appeared, at times, to take centre stage, while for some, professional rugby was deemed a cancer that was destroying the sport, requiring action to be taken. That was the motivation for those within the corridors of RFU power who wanted to regain control of a sport they deemed to be teetering on the brink of an abyss. Having accepted the role of CEO in 1998, Baron was the obvious focus for the amateur ire and he had to fight numerous battles – winning most of them, it must be said.

The biggest challenge to Baron's position as CEO came in the early 2000s when Graeme Cattermole, who had become RFU chairman, decided it was time to discuss Baron's performance. He is the man credited with what a small group inside the RFU referred to as 'Project St George'. Baron said: 'I am not a shrinking violet when it comes to fighting my corner and it was important to be single-minded and persuasive with council, who didn't [in his view] always see the bigger picture. You have to stick to your guns and if you don't have a clear vision and deliver results then you cannot carry the broader body of the game with you – particularly the elected council members. There were various battles with Graeme Cattermole, who was RFU chairman for a while, and in the early years Fran Cotton, too. There was an attempt by Cattermole to remove me as CEO – that was one of the battles I had to fight around 2002–3.

'Did I ever think, "Is this worth it?" No, but I think my wife thought that at various times during that period. However, the majority of people on the council are sensible and listen to rational arguments and can be carried. At the end of the day, Cattermole went and that speaks for itself. I always believe that council will come to the right decision, even if it is in a rather tortuous manner! There were battles all the time but I was paid to win those battles and deliver the right end result. You cannot let a series of bad results on the pitch affect your long-term plan and in the end it didn't derail it.'

For his own part, Cattermole would no doubt insist that he was right to raise concerns raised by some in relation to Baron's role. Cattermole resigned his role as chairman of the RFU management board in 2004, with a council resolution reaffirming its support for Baron but accepting his resignation with regret and acknowledging the contribution he had made to the game. Paul Vaughan, appointed by Baron as commercial director of the RFU to boost Twickenham Stadium's revenue, insists that there were at least two moves by a small group to oust his former boss during those turbulent days in the 2000s and that rugby administrators still struggle to fully understand the link between sponsors and the game. He explained, 'There was an attempt – two in fact – to oust Francis from his role as CEO. It was, I believe, called Operation St George and designed to replace him and I got to hear about this because in this kind of thing there is always counter-intelligence. You can imagine how uncomfortable the situation was in meetings when you knew that certain people were not telling the truth. This kind of attitude is something I had experienced from people in the Union when I was a sponsor of the game. They would adopt the stance of, "Thanks for the sponsorship cheque and don't bother us again." They wanted the money but no involvement from the sponsor.'

The clearest example of this came when European rugby administrators set up the Heineken Cup, and would show that hidebound Union attitudes were not confined to Twickenham. The company that put its name to what became the outstanding club rugby competition in the world expected to be greeted with open arms. How wrong they were, as Vaughan, who at the time was working for the sponsors, recalled: 'I remember when we had the first Heineken Cup final and I suggested that Miles Templeman, our top man, should present the trophy. The response from the organisers of the competition was, "Oh, no, you can't do that." We also had to sit in the second row of the committee box at the final at Cardiff Arms Park, not in the front row, for the culmination of a competition we had funded. They just didn't get it and you could argue that while a lot has changed for the better, some people in the game still don't get it.'

Having battled the amateur ethos from 1998, Francis Baron retired early from his role in 2010 to be replaced by John Steele, who lasted barely a year amid internal warfare over the appointment of a performance director. Eventually, Ian Ritchie was appointed in December 2011, having previously held the high-profile role as CEO of the All England Club, who run the Wimbledon Championships. He agreed to become the point man for the RFU, but the 'governance' of the Union in the professional era is still being sorted out.

Chapter Eleven

Twickenham makes BBC history and Jeremy Clarkson rips up the pitch

Twickenham provided the backdrop for broadcasting history in 1927 when the BBC set up a small wooden booth for Henry Blythe Thornhill (Teddy) Wakelam, who played at the stadium for Harlequins in 1912, to provide the first commentary on a rugby international – England's 11–9 win over Wales. The *Radio Times* produced a special 'map' of the Twickenham pitch that was broken down into four sections – A, B, C and D – with another member of the BBC team in the commentary box telling the listeners which area the ball had moved into. One of the few pieces of advice Wakelam was given before that first broadcast was 'don't swear', and he handled the pressure of this step into the broadcasting unknown with calm assuredness.

This was not surprising given the calibre of the man in front of the heavy and rather cumbersome microphone that momentous day at Twickenham. Wakelam had joined Quins in 1911 and was up at Cambridge until the outbreak of the First World War, but did not win a blue. He served in Gallipoli and on the Western Front, twice being wounded and mentioned in dispatches. He was temporarily blinded by mustard gas in 1918 but recovered well enough to return to playing with the club in 1919 and then assumed the role of club secretary until 1923, having captained them the previous season. His army service continued after the war and he assisted Marshal Foch in transporting General Haller's Polish Army home through Germany; while he then resigned his commission, he did continue a connection with the army, becoming a territorial with the Royal Engineers. He would see service during the Second World War in the Middle East, despite being forty-seven years old. Wakelam was well known by then thanks to his broadcasting career, which had blossomed to include covering boxing, cricket and tennis, along with the Tidworth Tattoo. A week after he had provided the first commentary at Twickenham he was alongside C.A. Lewis for the first live broadcast of a football match, describing the contest between Arsenal and Sheffield United. While covering Wimbledon in the 1930s his notes caught fire but he remained calm throughout the incident!

The first televised rugby international at Twickenham came in 1938 when England entertained Scotland, while the Empire was given a glimpse of what an international was like through the lenses of the Pathé News camera crews, who filmed from fixed positions. The number of cameras remained limited by technology into the 1970s, when just five were used to illustrate the magical commentaries of Cliff Morgan and Bill McLaren.

It is in stark contrast to the television coverage now delivered at Twickenham by a wide range of broadcasters, including the BBC, Sky and BT Sport. Now, the television operation which sends images of Twickenham Stadium around the world is at the very cutting edge of sports broadcasting. Paul Davies, BBC Sport executive producer, believes the service provided has a direct lineage from Wakelam's days. He said: 'It is an amazing legacy and the principle hasn't changed – we are still trying to give people the best seat in the house. For a major Six Nations match at Twickenham, for example England versus Wales, you will have the BBC as host broadcaster, S4C from Wales, along with BBC Wales plus French, Italian and Irish television partners who are all showing the match in their areas. They all have various demands which vary from having their own camera to supplement what we are putting out plus their own commentary positions and presentation points, along with flash interview areas. It is quite a complex setup and not even a World Cup will be busier. For a game with Wales there will be up to twenty-five cameras.'

The evolution of television coverage – radio is by its nature more restricted – has been at breakneck speed in the last ten years. There are concerns that the manner of the picture gathering is in danger of becoming too intrusive, with Twickenham now featuring the 'Spidercam', which sees wires attached to four corners of the roof to enable a camera to be sent flying above the pitch. The camera can drop to ground level and then follow the flight of a kick at goal. There have been experiments with a drone carrying a camera powered by mini-propellers, and every week appears to offer a new gimmick. Coverage at Twickenham revolves around the fixed and mobile cameras that are in the hands of camera operators.

'Different groups of cameras have different roles,' explained Davies. 'Your core cameras operate from the television gantry and many people are very familiar with this, and there will be two cameras doing wide and tight shots; then there will be a camera above the tunnel to get the personality shots of the players; the next group will be found in each of the four corners and with the TMO [television match official], you use these for "foot in touch" and also tries in the corners. Those are cameras that are super-slow motion for replays; then you have cameras on the 22m line at the same height as the main gantry and one will keep the referee in the picture to get his reaction and decisions; there are high end cameras at the top of the North and South Stands and we have been working closely with the RFU for plans to put in new floodlights that will have an impact on matches by creating a natural light for the pitch.

'We used to put scaffolding around those cameras in the seats but they have their own bespoke positions now. There is also a high analysis camera which is useful for the studio discussion and offers a bird's-eye view, and it is operated from the control scanner vehicle. There are pitch-side hand-held cameras on either side, basically keeping up with play like a touch judge. They are typically radio cameras without the need for cables and these can have hi-motion replay that is really super-slow capability. There are also cameras on the East Stand middle-level gantry to capture blind-side breaks on the pitch and also help give the best possible view of kicks at goal and to touch. Spidercam has become a really good tool with those overhead shots of the scrum and also with kicks at goal because it can travel with the ball. The Spidercam is operated by a team of four people who set it up on each corner to allow it to travel in any direction and height. For the match, there is a pilot and a cameraman and it's quite a skill to allow them to work together.'

All these pictures have to be drawn together to provide a coherent coverage of the match, with the director needing to find a balance between the broad canvas that allows the armchair fan to understand the ebb and flow of the game and the close-ups that put the viewer at the heart of the action. The pictures are all fed into what is called a scanner vehicle parked in the large television compound in the northwest area of the stadium; those handling the flow of information and images never actually see the live match. 'There are six other trucks which take all the feeds from the cameras and it's all there on a bank of screens along with analysis kit, replay machines and graphics. Twickenham has permanent power on site and is well geared up, but we bring backup generators in case the main source goes down.

'In recent times,' continued Davies, 'Twickenham has put in their own fibre optic cables and the corner cameras are able to just plug into those junctions around the pitch to get the pictures back to the scanner. Twickenham is very advanced in this area and they are also able to use them for concerts. The stadium has been tidied up because you don't have all of those cables everywhere. In total we would have more than a hundred people on site producing the television coverage of an international. The sound is also very important with technology allowing surround sound, and a lot of kit goes into capturing the amazing atmosphere for the fans sitting at home and also picking up the referee's microphone.'

Thankfully there were only limited sound and vision facilities to capture one of the more bizarre attempts to get exposure for the Emirate Airline London Sevens staged at Twickenham in 2011. The promo film was based – very loosely – on *Baywatch* and featured members of the RFU, along with the ground staff, reprising the roles of the famous stars, including the Hoff. In the lead role was head groundsman Keith Kent in a red women's bathing suit that was more Ann Widdecombe than Pamela Anderson!

Real film stars have been regular attendees at Twickenham rugby matches, with the infamous pair of Richard Harris and Peter O'Toole taking every opportunity to enjoy a day out and help boost bar profits. There was even a visit in the 1970s by the most famous couple in the world at that time, Richard Burton and Elizabeth Taylor, although that appearance ended in some controversy when a steward looking after the Internationals Bar asked them to leave the premises. He pointed out that as neither was a former rugby international they had no right to be enjoying a drink in that bar. Rules are rules!

Diana Dors, Britain's answer to Marilyn Monroe (well, that's what her publicity machine insisted), and Bernard

Cribbins were given a rather warmer welcome by the Twickenham staff when they took part in filming *The Counterfeit Constable*, a 1964 French comedy film directed by Robert Dhéry and Pierre Tchernia that also featured Ronald Fraser and Arthur Mullard. Its French title is *Allez France!* The plot revolves around a French rugby supporter in England for a match at Twickenham who is knocked out and loses two teeth. He goes to the dentist and, while waiting, the fan somehow ends up wearing the uniform of another patient, a police officer. He saves, by chance, Diana Dors (playing herself) and is congratulated by his chiefs, who take him for a true police officer (although he doesn't speak a word of English).

What made this film truly memorable for Harold Clark, the clerk of works who had started his job earlier that year, was the comings and goings near the North Stand. He spotted a young woman who kept disappearing behind the stand with various members of the cast and crew. It transpired that she was a prostitute plying her trade at the stadium.

One of Twickenham's most-watched appearances on screen came courtesy of the world-famous *Top Gear* motoring programme, which introduced 'car rugby' to the stadium's long list of sporting guises. When it was initially announced that cars would be careering over the sacred turf chasing an unfeasibly large rugby ball, the traditionalists assumed it was a joke. In fact, it was another example of Twickenham's forward thinking and eye for a publicity opportunity. With the pitch being dug up in 2012 to allow a new Desso system to be installed, trashing the old pitch with cars no longer became a problem.

Top Gear presenters Jeremy Clarkson and James May were joined by other experienced drivers to make up two teams, and the BBC filmed the 'match', which was expected to reach a worldwide TV audience of 400m. The RFU was aware that Clarkson was a big England rugby fan, and contacted the programme. The RFU approach was basically: 'Our pitch is being totally relaid and with that in mind, would you fancy messing about on the pitch the night before the diggers come in?' The idea was to suggest the *Top Gear* team had somehow avoided security at the most famous rugby stadium in the world and managed to drive family cars onto the pitch for an impromptu game of car rugby. *Top Gear* loved the idea, developed it into a 'car rugby match' that could be played on the pitch and filmed it with the stadium floodlights providing the illumination for scenes never before witnessed at Twickenham Stadium. The fact that the evening was wet only enhanced the image of the pitch, which had for years been carefully manicured on an hourly basis, being carved up, with grass and turf flying everywhere. The end result was spectacular, with viewers perplexed at how Clarkson and the boys had managed it, and how and why the RFU – that most conservative of sporting bodies – had let it happen. Needless to say, those within the Union who had not been in on the ruse were also stunned to discover that *Top Gear* had driven Kia Cee'ds and Kia Sportages all over the Twickenham Stadium pitch with the Stig as referee in a Vauxhall Astra police car. Both sets of vehicles and the pitch were in a terrible state by the end of the match, which featured stock car racing-style crashes and impressive conversions from in front of the posts by May and Clarkson.

Clarkson's first conversion effort, attempted by driving his car at the ball which was perched on a large tee – appeared successful until the ball crashed into the crossbar and rebounded into play. The crossbar survived this assault, but in fact insurance had been taken out to cover damage to the two sets of posts, as they assumed it would be needed in case one of the cars collided with the uprights.

Groundsman Keith Kent didn't wait around to see his turf churned up by various sensibly priced family cars and headed home. His colleagues Ian Ayling and Andy Muir opted to remain and enjoy this highly usual spectacle, and it would turn out to be one of the most frightening and exhilarating days of their lives. Kent takes up the story: 'I left Ian and Andy and they sent me some pictures and it was great publicity. We insured the posts for £4,500 and how they didn't hit them I don't know! When Ian and Andy went into the dressing rooms at half-time, they approached the Stig and asked if he could take them for a ride. He didn't speak – as usual – but pointed to a car and they got in. They went to the South Stand end and he did a bit of a doughnut between the posts and then set off down the east wing – off the grass onto the tarmac – and was hitting 60mph by the time he came back onto the pitch and did a handbrake turn. He actually went over the pitch and careered over the little wall and Ian and Andy thought they were dead! But just when they thought the Stig was going to hit the wall of the stand, he changed gear and set off again, doing 60mph in about three seconds up the west wing. When the Stig stopped, the lads said they got out absolutely shaking and frightened to death, but loved every moment of the experience. The Stig was driving a police car in the match and the instruction from the other television show they had borrowed it from was, "Don't damage the police car, we need it next week."'

He didn't.

Chapter Twelve

Twickenham tickets – mine's in the dog!

The next time you get a Twickenham match ticket in your hand, try to find the six security features that have been devised to thwart forgers. Pat Murphy, the RFU ticket officer, can find five, but the sixth and final one is not even known to her – the most important person in Twickenham's elaborate ticket system. 'When we changed ticket supplier we wanted a lot of security within the ticket and there are six. They include embossing, numbering, hologram and the one I don't know about. I asked for an extra one because it is a safeguard against anything going wrong,' said Murphy, who is one of three vital past and present members of the ticketing team to have guided the Union through tough and challenging times. The other two are former ticket officer Richard Ankerson and Lisa Prior, who has worked in the office since she was sixteen. Together they have solved seemingly insurmountable problems, saved the 1991 World Cup final from becoming a disaster and changed the system from one that revolved around endless boxes and handwritten orders to the computerised operation that now handles all kinds of events at the stadium.

A total of 51 per cent of Twickenham's international rugby tickets go to clubs, with the rest allocated to the opposition, debenture holders, corporate box holders, schools and referee societies, among others. For Six Nations matches the number handed out to the opposition is based on a reciprocal arrangement; for example, with France the arrangement is 7,500, while for Scotland and Wales games it is around 6,500. For Lansdowne Road the figure is 5,500, while a southern hemisphere team at Twickenham for an autumn match would receive an allocation of 4,000.

Today the stadium has various prices for different sections in the three-tier arena, but for many years you bought a ticket for a particular stand and found whatever seat was free. This sounds like rugby's version of a budget airline, where you could end up sitting next to anyone and your mates would be scattered all over the aircraft. Given that the first international was staged in 1910, it is remarkable to record that the one-price stand seating was only abandoned in 1975, when the RFU had to increase seating prices and felt it was time to delineate between what could be described as the 'best' seats and those further towards the ends of the three stands. Terrace tickets, particularly in the large south area, caused their own particular problems, as we shall see. The takings for that first international in 1910 were £2,250 and all the money went into the RFU coffers, which was the whole point of ending the practice of taking games to venues such as Crystal Palace.

Another important date in the history of Twickenham ticketing is 1953, when England played Wales. This was the first all-ticket game and thousands of fans turned up hoping, as usual, to pay on the gate to get in, only to find the new system in place. Tom Prentice in his letter to the RFU museum said, 'Counting machines were used in all entrances and on the South Terrace it was found that uniformed gatekeepers from an agency were accepting ten-shilling notes instead of tickets on a "frighteningly dangerous scale". Grandstand seats cost ten shillings and bench seats, called ground tickets, five shillings.' George Young, who began in 1946, was the ticket officer and had a part-time lady to help him, and a couple of people who came in during the season when needed; the ticket operation involved 50 turnstiles and 120 gatemen. One year in four there would be an England game and a London Counties match before Christmas, plus the final England trial along with the two Five Nations matches. Added to the list were three Services games and the Middlesex Sevens. The whole process of ground control was made that much tougher by the need to sell thousands of terrace tickets.

With a new system in place for Young and his small team of helpers to deal with, the process was both slow and time-consuming. Applications were entered in the cash book by hand and, on one occasion, the office cleaners at Watford

RFC binned their entire ticket allocation by mistake and duplicates needed to be issued by hand under the command of Young in the ticket office. The system was still this archaic when Richard Ankerson joined the ticket office in 1974, after spotting an advert in the *Daily Telegraph* offering a job as assistant ticket officer at the RFU.

Ankerson explained his recruitment in the wake of the Turkish Airlines disaster, when a McDonnell Douglas DC-10 crashed outside Paris on 3 March 1974, killing all 346 people on board. The flight's second leg, from Paris to Heathrow, was normally underbooked, but due to a strike by British European Airways employees, many London-bound travellers who had been stranded at Orly were booked on Flight 981. Among them were seventeen English rugby players who had attended the France vs England match the previous day: 'There had been the Turkish Airlines disaster and the French said they would come over to play England to help raise funds for the families of those who had been killed. The workload that put on George Young meant that Bob Weighill, the secretary, decided that kind of pressure could not be inflicted upon George again at short notice and so I became the first assistant ticket officer.'

It appears that members of the England team were lucky to avoid being caught up in the tragedy. The *Citizen* newspaper in Gloucester reported in 1974:

> Rugby Union officials decided that the team should return home together. The players were called off the [Turkish Airlines] plane, others took their seats, and as the monster jet flew out, they boarded a

Pakistani Airlines plane which brought them safely home. The quartet was England and Gloucestershire skipper John Pullin, England selector and Gloucester fruiterer Peter Ford, Gloucester prop Mike Burton, and club colleague John Watkins. Mr Burton said today that several of the team and their wives actually got on the plane, but were called off when Air Commodore Bob Weighill, secretary of the RU, and Lt.-Col. Dennis Morgan, his administrative secretary, made the fortunate decision that they should stay in one party and return on a later flight.

Ankerson, who succeeded George Young in 1981 and would stay in post until 2003, continued: 'George did the first international after the Second World War and so that meant there were only two ticket officers from the end of the war until the twenty-first century. Alf Wright did the job before George and stayed in place during the Second World War. When I started there were 34,000 seats and 36,000 standing tickets – the South and North Terraces and East and West had standing in front of the stands. We had problems with overcrowding in one Welsh match when people were coming in on the Friday and sleeping in the stand and also jumping the fences from the gardens of houses on Whitton Road. One game in 1980 against Wales was the worst atmosphere I had known and I would not have been surprised if there were five thousand more than there should have been on the terraces. The original plan for the replacement North Stand was for a terrace in front but that didn't happen after the Taylor report.'

Ankerson was shown how the ticket system operated, which involved manually writing down the orders from the clubs, universities and schools who were entitled to tickets; the amount of money deposited with the Union determined the number you would eventually receive. If a match, as often happened, was sold out, then the larger amount you lodged, the greater percentage of tickets you would earn. 'One financial institution cooked their own goose,' said Ankerson, 'because if we had given them the allocation they requested with the huge cheque that was deposited, they would have received one in three tickets for the stadium! The top-price ticket was thirty-five pounds and they put up a six-figure sum. That brought about a change in the allocation system. The clubs applied in the September and the RFU sat on this vast amount of money until December when we sent out the allocation of tickets and refunds.

'In 1991, when we were also dealing with the World Cup ticket allocation, Lisa – who had just had a baby – returned to the office and offered to look after the Five Nations ticket requests for later in the season. After about three days, Lisa said she wanted someone to help her go to the bank to get rid of some of the money that had come in for tickets. I asked, "How much have you got?" and Lisa replied, "I've got six-and-a-half-million pounds." The figures were that big so the system changed in the mid-1990s when we told the clubs what their maximum allocation could be and the RFU no longer sat on that huge amount of money.'

The ticket office in the build-up to a match during this period would resemble a sorting house, with boxes lined up along one wall containing the tickets for each stand. They were in bundles and had a colour to show which stand they were for, while the terrace tickets were another colour. One person would read out the allocation and other members of the team would select at random the relevant number of stand seats from each section, and they would all be bundled together and then sent out to the applicant.

'I started working out how many tickets had passed through my hands during nearly thirty years and I was amazed to find it was fourteen million!' added Ankerson, who is now based in Gloucestershire and is still helping sort out tickets – this time for the county organisation and looking after local leagues. 'The manual system was massively time-consuming and on occasions a box would be lifted up and a few tickets found underneath! If I wanted to see England play I would go to Paris or Dublin but not Twickenham, because I wanted to be around if there were any problems. Lisa started in 1982 and until 1991 we had gatemen who would arrive to be paid during the game and we also had to count up money for tickets sold on the day. The Middlesex Sevens was a huge attraction and all the seats were sold and the standing area attendance was reduced to about 10,000, which meant they were a third full to allow for movement and the setting up of their own bars. The honorary stewards were given lunch in their own restaurant and then went to their positions in the stands and were not paid. Gatemen were paid but didn't get lunch, and an eye was kept on that area to make sure people weren't paying to get in,' he said, referring to the habit of some gatemen to accept cash that then went into their own pocket. 'When the South Stand hospitality boxes opened a security firm took over to offer a smarter operation. We also got rid of the stadium turnstiles; some went to local clubs who needed some crowd control while a lot were sold off for scrap. Some seasons were very difficult to deal with because of different capacities; the lowest it got was around 54,000 for the match with South Africa in 1992 when it poured with rain onto those people in the lower tier of the East Stand, which was all that had been built at that point. We had moved to the proportional system for distribution based on club membership, rather than how much money you could muster.'

Pat Murphy remembers all of the boxes and the endless counting required to keep the ticket system working in the pre-computer period. Like Ankerson, she had been working in a local bank and was looking for a change of job. 'I used to work at NatWest and Richard had previously worked with Lloyds. One of the RFU staff came in and said, "You look cheesed off," and I said I was and were there any jobs at your place? The old-fashioned banking had lots of similarities with what was happening at the ticket office, particularly reconciliation. We still adopt the same policies about reconciling work at the end of the day. In 1989 it was still a manual system off a plan and handwritten to a large degree. When we got the tickets we checked it against what you would call these days a spreadsheet. The plans were handed down because the stadium had not changed for a long time. It was a very manual system with tickets having a different colour for each stand and a red line if it was a different price. We would put the tickets in boxes that corresponded to the various stands and they ran along the length of the ticket office. You randomly selected the tickets according to the request. It took weeks to sort out.' And as well as that there were Varsity Match tickets and one autumn international a year to deal with.

She continued, 'We used to have a West Stand office and we handled a large amount of cash. These days there aren't that many cheques because of direct debit payments etc. Credit cards had just started being used and so cash or cheque was the norm. We had a police presence around the office and all the money could be put in a night safe.

'We started to look at computerised ticketing just before the 1991 World Cup and the Save & Prosper International tickets were produced by De La Rue and we overprinted in-house. We had a number of forged tickets before a computerised system was adopted and we had some about six years ago for England versus Ireland coming through Liverpool. We have no scanning system and it was only spotted when the people went to their seat and found someone else already there. We only had a few and I think that the myth that you cannot get hold of a ticket for a Twickenham international means that if someone is selling a ticket in a pub you would be very wary. Tickets can get stolen in the post or lost and they are replaced.'

The ticket office's 1980s home in the West Stand area saw it also take on the unwanted role of enquiry office. Besides dealing with endless queries about lost tickets and last-minute attempts to purchase the opportunity to witness that day's match, Ankerson and his staff found themselves also handling disturbing news – without any specialist training. With nowhere else to go, the police turned to the ticket office to try to contact fans in the ground who needed to be given bad news. Ankerson said, 'For many years – Dudley Wood put a stop to this when he arrived in 1986 – it was our responsibility to man the enquiry office. There was no police office and it fell to us to deal with ghastly things like getting a message to someone in the ground that a family member had died in a car crash and that sort of thing. If we couldn't work out where they were sitting we had to put out a PA message and then break the terrible news when the person came to the office. If the police brought the bad news then an officer would be there but if the RFU was contacted direct, then it fell to us to deal with it.' Fortunately it wasn't always bad news. 'There were happy messages about the birth of a child as well! Dudley recognised we shouldn't be dealing with that and before the 1991 World Cup a security department was set up to handle those situations.'

Very few, if any, tickets are actually sold on the day of an international due to the chaos that would cause. But the desperate need to get a ticket for Twickenham leads to all kinds of weird and wonderful excuses being given to the ticket office staff to try to have them make an exception. Over the many years he was ticket officer, Ankerson heard them all. 'People would come and say, "My brother has just decided to come over from South Africa/New Zealand/ Australia and it would be fantastic if we could make his trip special." On one occasion there was a member of the House of Lords who arrived on match day and picked up duplicate tickets that had been lost when he left his briefcase at Victoria station, and then he tried to get some more by pulling rank on match day. There were occasions when it got a bit hairy and we did have to call security, and on some occasions the police, to remove people.'

Pat Murphy has kept a souvenir of one recent excuse for the reissue of a ticket. She was sent the bits of ticket that the person's dog had chewed up, hence the need to have a duplicate. Other tickets are damaged through sheer incompetence, including the man who tried to iron his wet ticket dry and only succeeded in turning the heat-sensitive paper totally black. 'There are regular excuses for why they have lost tickets and they haven't changed over the years, with "It's the wife's fault" one of the most common. She threw them away or put them into the washing machine. We get tickets that are destroyed in a matrimonial dispute when the wife has discovered the husband is going to Twickenham with a girlfriend. People tell you – a stranger – these very personal stories because they are desperate to see the match. We have had lots of "tickets eaten by the dog" stories and during the 2014 Six Nations someone sent in by post these pieces of a ticket that had been well and truly chewed. Email has made things easier because people can send a message ahead explaining why they haven't got their ticket and we can reissue it, but we still get frantic supporters turning up at the ticket office on match days. When I brief the staff before a home game with Ireland I do say that the Irish fans are going to spin some wonderful stories in a bid to get a ticket for the game. They are a lot of fun.

'We have been successful for a number of decades in selling out tickets for matches at Twickenham but there are challenges to regularly filling the stadium. Ticketmaster are our call centre and they can move volumes of tickets but we still give priority to our members and club, along with debenture holders. When we know a match isn't going to sell out we go on public sale through Ticketmaster. These days we also have our England Rugby Supporters Club with 23,000 members and they pay a subscription and enter a ballot for some matches. For England versus Australia in November 2013 around 12,000 tickets were sold through Ticketmaster and there are a number of reasons [why a match doesn't sell out]: cost of tickets, three matches in a row on successive weekends and the cost of travel. There is also so much more for people to spend their money on and what confirms to me that the game is so strong is the number of sold-out matches we do have at Twickenham in the season. When you see where we were in New Zealand at the 2011 World Cup and how we came back with our tails between our legs and where we are now, then you can see how much hard work has been put in to change the atmosphere which is now really, really good. When we have lost and lost badly, we get complaints about all kinds of things coming to the ticket office, but when we win it's all fantastic and hardly any negative comments. We have 359 free tickets for wheelchair users and a helper which means there are more than 600 in the stadium on match days; that is run on a priority system for people who have been hurt playing rugby and is a ballot system.'

For Murphy, the use of new technology is something Twickenham has to embrace, with ticketless entry one of the looming developments. Fans will be able to show their ticket bar code on their phone to a sensor at the gate to get entry, something designed to keep the stadium at the forefront of technology. 'Our capacity is just under 82,000 with 78,392 stadium seats and the rest is made of hospitality. Where the big TV screens were put in that took out 200 seats at either end of the stadium and we are looking to move them from the seats and aim to suspend the screen above the pitch like the Millennium Stadium. Rugby is now way up in the list of popular tickets and we still don't get lots of problems with forgeries, which probably says a lot about the type of supporters we have and their desire to see the game. There will be automatic turnstiles and we will not need, at that point, as many security features on the ticket. The plan is to move away from a paper ticket to things like a smart card, print-at-home facility, mobile technology and RFU ID.'

For Ankerson, that kind of technological jump forward only heightens the wonderment that a system that, for so long relied upon the manual skills of a small group of dedicated staff, kept getting it so right over so many years. Now, he can sit back and enjoy matches at Twickenham without worrying if everyone got into the ground. He added, 'Lisa, myself and Pat saw incredible changes at Twickenham and when I disappeared in 2003 and handed over to Pat, it was very smooth. Pat worked out that during our time together she had spent massively more hours with me than her husband! Looking back at all the rebuilding and what we dealt with during my time, I take a lot of pride at what we all achieved. I now go to Twickenham as a fan, having been honoured to be given two tickets for the committee area in the West Stand for every match, and for the first time I can have a pint. For some time it didn't seem right and I still had the urge to go around the ground checking everything was OK.'

Paul Vaughan, the former RFU business operations director, is adamant that tickets on the black market for every Twickenham match siphon off around £1m that could be ploughed back into the game. The battle to control the number of tickets that get into the 'wrong' hands was one he constantly fought during his ten-year period at Twickenham. The 2012 London Olympics benefitted from special Government legislation that made it easier to control the black market, but for organisations like the RFU and the All England Lawn Tennis Club, which organises the Wimbledon Championships, the problem will not go away. In fact, it is now an online headache more than an unwanted practice involving men walking up and down Whitton Road muttering, 'Buy and sell any tickets,' out of the side of their mouths. These men are still present, however, and can be found in Rome trying to ply their illegal trade for England's away game with Italy, and some even made it down to Australia to try to cash in on the 2003 World Cup tournament. There are police restrictions in place designed to keep known touts out of the area of the stadium once they have been spotted and warned, but with so much happening online these days, it is a problem that is increasingly hard to counter.

Vaughan told me, 'It was difficult to gauge the unofficial market but we always believed it was worth around a million pounds. When I started we thought about eight-thousand tickets were getting onto the black market, and we cut this by half pretty swiftly.' Apparently, the tougher sanctions on clubs and individuals that allowed their tickets to reach the touts had an effect. 'The black market still gets fed and they are, obviously, still getting tickets from somewhere. The only tickets which have legal protection are football ones for safety reasons, and we saw during the 2012 London Olympics that the government passed a special bill because the IOC insist this happens. We have tried to work with various governments to try and persuade them to bring something in to protect our ticket sales, along with those of the music business and other sports. With a club-based system you are not dealing with the end users – the club is the middleman, who has to control its members.' He thinks that without government legislation the only way to tackle the problem is to join forces with the online ticket agencies and legitimise them, but that is not an ideal solution. 'The Premiership clubs are using StubHub to move tickets online and that means money is not staying in the game.'

For Richard Ankerson, getting information about potential problems with forged tickets was always a priority, particularly if there were rumours about dodgy tickets being available. Prices coming down on the black market was an indicator he looked for, but another way of finding out if his match day was going to involve a lot of irate fans trying to sit in seats already occupied by someone with a forged ticket was to get to the touts himself. Having spent so long in charge of the ticket office, Ankerson knew many of the touts because for much of his time, unlike today, they were present in the street rather than on the end of a telephone line or working a computer.

Ankerson explained: 'Some of the touts were rather unpleasant men, but one or two had a bit of honour among thieves and were helpful in certain situations. One of the most annoying situations with forged tickets revolved around a call we took from a police officer from north London in the lead-up to a match with France, and he said they had reason to believe forgeries were in circulation. My heart sank because we were so close to the game and I knew that black-market prices were astonishingly high for the game, which suggested there weren't any around. The officer said he had a good source and was adamant about the forgeries but before we put in extra precautions and barriers to ensure tickets could be closely checked, I rang a tout in Shepherd's Bush and said, "Is there something going on that I don't know about for the French game?" He insisted there were no forgeries and said he would check it out and get back to me the next day, which was the Wednesday before the match. Good as gold, he came back to me and said he had been around all the offices and agencies and the various blokes he knew and there were no forgeries. I told him that if some turned up he had better not cross my path again. I told Lisa I was going to believe the tout and not the police although, I have to admit, I didn't sleep very well on the night before the match. On match day, I kept walking around the turnstiles checking for any problems and everything went smoothly. On the Monday I rang the officer back and said we hadn't had any of the forgeries he had claimed were going to be a problem. Remarkably, he said: "Oh, yes, it was for a football match at Wembley." He hadn't bothered to ring me back with this very important information and thank goodness for our friendly tout who saved us a lot of extra security costs.'

One of the positives about the decision to end terrace places at Twickenham was the ability to stamp out forgeries. Tickets for these areas were very popular, leading to money-making schemes by people who had access to printing presses that produced genuine-looking terrace tickets. Ankerson admitted, 'We had a bad run in the late 1970s with people forging standing place tickets and some were very good. This led to a meeting about the ticket security. We then used UV lights to check they were genuine and we had a pretty good idea if there were forged ones around because the black-market price would drop. That was one giveaway. No matter how good the forgery was, there was always someone around the game who would ring up and say they had bought a ticket and they felt something wasn't right. It was always a great help.'

Pat Murphy, the current ticket officer at Twickenham, is at the forefront of the battle with cyber-touts. The ticket department has to monitor movement of tickets online because it has become such a key market for those who want to move tickets that need to be traced back to the original owner. The RFU operates a system that penalises the club or person whose name is printed on the ticket. If a ticket is discovered on the black market with the identifying name, action is taken and high-profile players have been caught up in the crackdown. Owen Farrell, the Lions and England No. 10, found himself in danger of losing his future allocations when a ticket in his name was sold on the black market in February 2014. Farrell was absolved of any wrongdoing after being able to show he had no knowledge of the route that the ticket had taken after he had, in good faith, supplied it to a friend. The £70 ticket was sold on the viagogo website to an Ireland fan living in Northern Ireland for £440. England flanker James Haskell had his allocation suspended for three matches after he was found to have contravened the ticket terms and conditions for matches at Twickenham five years ago. In 2012, the RFU secured a landmark judgment in its long-standing dispute with viagogo, one of the biggest secondary ticket brokers, following an eighteen-month legal battle. It defeated viagogo in the Supreme Court, which agreed with the High Court's decision to grant an order requiring the identities of people selling tickets on viagogo's website to be revealed. Murphy said: 'We spend a lot of hours policing the secondary market and we do take a small number of tickets back and sell on the day. We manage a queue on match days with our security staff to make sure there are no touts and we give them a heads-up. If there aren't going to be any tickets, we tell the fans it's better to head off to the pub to watch the game.

'Some of the touts appear abroad, including being in Australia for the 2003 World Cup, and they have a whole network supporting their operations. Before you would see the tout with a ticket in their hand but now they are more likely to be on a mobile phone and use runners. The introduction of the internet has changed a lot of what happens and touts can run their operation from the comfort of their armchair. We operate in conjunction with Trading Standards and the Metropolitan Police an antisocial exclusion zone that runs from Barclays Bank in Twickenham town centre right up to the stadium. Police will move active touts outside that area and if they come back in, they will take action.'

The need for the Unions to shift tickets that are not selling through normal outlets is mounting, with the game's finances so stretched, particularly in Scotland. The Scottish RFU have taken a dramatic step in deciding to work with viagogo and the company is always keen to emphasise that it is legal to re-sell tickets in the UK and that every purchase from its website is guaranteed. However, Murphy explained: 'Scotland have an arrangement with viagogo, which is something we wouldn't entertain, and also have bundled-up tickets which means for, say, Scotland versus England you had to buy tickets for a number of other Murrayfield games, which opens up potential problems. A number of ticket bundles were sold to a particular person and I was asked by someone in Scotland if I knew the name and it was a tout who worked out of the Leicester area!'

One of the biggest headaches the Twickenham ticket office faced came in 1991 when England reached the Rugby World Cup final against Australia. Richard Ankerson and Pat Murphy had been drafted in to help run the ticket operation for what was only the second-ever World Cup. The first had been played in New Zealand four years earlier and the whole concept was still in its infancy – and so was the ticketing operation. For Ankerson in particular, there were potential problems that he dreaded, and being handed back tickets for a high-profile match with very little time to distribute them was top of his list. As it turned out, he had every reason to be worried and only quick thinking on the part of the RFU's ticket officer saved the final from being played in front of thousands of empty seats. It seems remarkable to think that the biggest game in England's rugby history came so close to being a PR disaster.

Here is how the debacle unfolded in Ankerson's words:

We had computers put into the ticket office the year before the World Cup in 1991 and it was accepted that the various Union ticket officers – the Cup also saw games played in France, Wales, Scotland and Ireland – would do their own matches and we had a few meetings, although it was our Cup as hosts. The real headache wasn't the demand from fans, it was the Cup organisers totally overestimating the number of tickets needed for official travel groups and hospitality, and even the size of the press box. I said we could live with all of that if there was an agreed date when we would get any tickets back to be redistributed. In the last ten days of the tournament, and particularly after the two semi-finals, we were swamped in the office with returned tickets for England versus Australia and we couldn't have banks of empty seats for the final. I would think we had up to 3,000 tickets returned and at the start of the week of the final I decided we would have to start getting rid of them by offering tickets to clubs away from London and leave the clubs in and around the capital till later in the week.

Thankfully, it was the old amateur days and the idea was we would send tickets to the big regional clubs like Leicester, Gloucester, Bristol and Moseley and ask them to distribute them to their combination clubs. I bounced this idea off my old mate Terry Tandy at Gloucester, having told the clubs for two years they wouldn't get more than two tickets for the final. I rang Terry and asked, 'How many tickets for the World Cup final do you think you can get rid of?' His reply was, 'How many are you talking about, six, ten . . .' I said, 'How about two hundred?' He didn't think that was feasible but took around a hundred and so on the Tuesday evening we had a fleet of courier motorbikes lined up at Twickenham outside the ticket office at 9 p.m. One went to Redruth, Plymouth and the southwest, another headed to Bristol and Gloucester, one to Moseley and the Birmingham clubs, also to Leicester, Northampton and Nottingham etc. The major club secretaries did extremely well getting all of those tickets distributed in such a short period of time. We got the money and the seats were filled. On the Friday, we had more tickets back and we contacted the London clubs and, not surprisingly, some thought it was a wind-up being twenty-four hours before the final. We rang one club and got the abrupt answer: 'F**k off!' It was an incredible logistical achievement and we should have been wined and dined for sorting it out rather than wound up.

Having pulled off a ticketing miracle in 1991, Ankerson realised there could be more problems for his team to deal with when the World Cup returned to Europe in 1999. Again, although the Cup organisers promised never to spread the tournament around so many countries again, they allowed matches to be scattered over Europe for the

1999 event hosted by Wales. Though the WRU was not found to be in any way responsible for the subsequent ticketing problems, the WRU ticket office suffered what its fellow Union ticket officials considered a 'meltdown' under the sheer weight of demand. 'In 1999 the Cup was hosted by Wales and we had the two semi-finals, but it was agreed that tickets should be printed by another organisation,' said Ankerson. 'I had a call from the SRU ticket officer saying he couldn't get through to the Welsh and BT told him the lines had been disconnected, and we both agreed to just get on with our own decisions. I rang Dublin and said this is what was happening with us while the good old French were doing their own thing. There was a problem with tickets being printed twice for the Twickenham semi-final. Around six hundred were printed twice for Sunday instead of Saturday *and* Sunday and there were empty seats for the first game. The clocks changed on the Sunday and I remember we became fully aware of this problem when two Kiwi lads came into the ticket office really early and they had the wrong block numbers and couldn't find their seats. Thankfully, we had time to work out what had happened and thanks to returned tickets we were able to seat everyone in the stadium who was affected. I didn't see either World Cup final and still haven't managed to see one!'

Chapter Thirteen

'Swing Low', Erica Roe

There are two moments in the history of Twickenham Stadium that have particularly caught the imagination – and the eye – of the fans who pack the stands. In 1988 a young Wasps wing called Chris Oti stunned Ireland with a hat-trick of tries that sent Twickenham into delirious celebration and helped the England team to a 35–3 victory on a day when they had lost their captain, Nigel Melville, to a broken leg. Melville, who went on to become director of rugby at Wasps and Gloucester before accepting the role of CEO of USA Rugby, has clear memories of that painful moment when his rugby career came to a premature end. Once Melville had departed, lock John Orwin took over the captaincy and the team needed inspiration. It came from Oti, whose playing style was described by team-mates as like watching a steel ball in a pinball machine. Opponents tried to grab the strongly built Cambridge University graduate but they just bounced off. His hat-trick was particularly warmly received by pupils from the Benedictine school Douai, who began singing the 150-year-old spiritual song 'Swing Low, Sweet Chariot', as they do for their first XV in celebration of tries at their school matches. With Oti, England's first black player for more than eighty years, having scored a hat-trick in just eleven amazing minutes, the pupils lucky enough to be in the ground started their school song. It was picked up by those standing near them, and before long the whole stadium was echoing to the sound of a joyous celebration that has become the national team's unofficial anthem. Wherever England play away from Twickenham, their fans deliver a rendition which normally elicits a cacophony of boos from the home supporters, particularly in France.

There were only cheers – along with gasps of astonishment – the day that Erica Roe wrote her name into the Twickenham Stadium history books courtesy of a topless streak during half-time in the England vs Australia game in 1982, an act that gave her the opportunity to introduce her forty-inch boobs to the wider world. It led to incredible publicity for her and an opportunity for Steve Smith, the England scrum half, who was playing that day and was enjoying a piece of half-time orange when he caught sight of Roe on the pitch.

Bill Beaumont, the England captain, was delivering a half-time team talk at that moment but noticed that no one was taking any interest in his inspirational words and appeared instead to be focusing on something happening over his shoulder. Beaumont, now the RFU chairman, takes up what has become a legendary after-dinner story delivered by Smith all over the country: 'Smithy tells the story really well, but we all mention it in speeches. I will never forget 2 January 1982 at approximately 2:44 p.m. – at half-time – and the story has become more apocryphal as time has gone on. The good version – the one Smithy tells – is that someone ran on the pitch and he turned to me in the half-time huddle and said, "Hey, Bill, there is a bloke on the pitch with your bum on his chest!" That is the one that does the dinner rounds and it's probably got better as time has moved on. At the time of the streak, we all stopped, looked and gulped at Erica Roe and were absolutely amazed. Everyone stopped, turned around and had a good look.

'At the time there were probably quite a few comments from the England players – "look at her, etc." – but I can't honestly remember Smithy coming out with that comment. He might have said it after the match because we only had five minutes on the pitch and John Clark would come with the white dish of orange slices. That was it. That was your rehydration at half-time – you gorged yourself on fourteen slices of orange and a piece of lemon for Brace [Peter Wheeler]. I know Brace liked a piece of lemon in a gin and tonic but I never knew it was his half-time fruit of choice until John Clark mentioned it for this book. Anyway, Brace didn't have any teeth so he was only ever going to suck the lemon! I don't know what happened to the guy in the gorilla suit and, surprisingly, he didn't get a great reception and I only have a recollection of one girl – Erica. The Australians got her to do a publicity shot in their hotel in Porthcawl in South Wales the following week, but there were terrible blizzards and she was stuck in the hotel with the Wallabies. I have met her once since that day, with the BBC's Ian Robertson who was doing an interview about the incident ten years after the event.'

Erica's intervention ensured that Clark would always remember the day, and it was the last thing he expected to witness on what was a very nervous occasion. Clark explained: 'I started in the role of clerk of works for the RFU on 1 January 1982 and the next day was the match with Australia where Erica streaked. I was in the middle of the pitch at half-time with the oranges – Peter Wheeler preferred a slice of lemon instead – and I came towards the captain Bill Beaumont. He looked straight over the top of me – which, given our differences in height, is not that difficult. I turned around and Erica was on the pitch with another very nice-looking girl and someone dressed as a gorilla who was running towards the England team. I remember wondering, do gorillas like oranges?'

Roe explained her appearance on the pitch – with ciga-rette hanging out of the side of her mouth – by stating that she had been drinking. 'I heard all this screaming and thought, "I have to get off, the second half is starting." But I quickly realised the roar was for me. Then I behaved like an egotistical bitch, put my arms in the air and went, "Yes! Hi!" That was fun,' she said when reflecting on the moment that captured the attention of the sporting nation and earned her a reported £8,000 from modelling. At the time of her streak she worked in a bookshop in Petersfield, Hampshire, later moving to Portugal to run an organic sweet-potato farm with her husband.

Roe was, in fact, the second streaker to make it onto the Twickenham pitch and become the focus of cameras to create a truly memorable photograph. The first to claim that honour was Michael O'Brien, an Australian, who had turned up to support a charity match in 1974 between England and France, to raise money for those affected by the Paris air crash earlier that year. An iconic photograph, which won Picture of the Year in *Life* magazine, shows O'Brien being led away by a police officer who has removed his helmet and placed it over the streaker's private parts. The policeman who arrested him, Bruce Perry, told the *Guardian* in 2006:

> The streaker had been drinking Fosters . . . and clearly he and some of his friends had an enjoyable time before the game drinking it. So he did it for a bet – he had to run across the pitch at half-time and touch the other side to win £10. I caught him just before he got there but when he explained the bet I let him touch the other side. It was a cold day and he didn't have anything to be proud of, but I didn't think twice about using my helmet. We took him down to the nick but he was back for the second half.

O'Brien didn't make any money for his streak as he was fined £10 – the same amount as the bet – by the court for his naked ambition. He returned to Australia and had a successful career as a fully clothed stockbroker.

Finding different ways to maximise the use of Twickenham Stadium has challenged RFU minds for decades. The most controversial has perhaps been the introduction of live concerts, featuring some of the most famous music acts in the world, with the Rolling Stones, Genesis, Lady Gaga and Rihanna among those to add the home of English rugby to their tour schedules. The RFU's first attempt at arranging a concert failed spectacularly against a backdrop of irate local residents and a local council that was unhappy with this proposed development. However, with each concert worth £1m to the Union, this was an income stream that needed to be added to the stadium's portfolio, and a charm offensive was launched that continues to this day to ensure concerts remain an integral part of the arena's future.

Richard Knight, the stadium director, is the key man when it comes to Twickenham's multi-use. It takes a week to set everything up for a concert and three days to dismantle everything, which means fitting concerts into an increasingly busy stadium schedule needs careful planning. Both Twickenham Stadium officials and the local residents were concerned about the potential noise impact of turning the home of rugby into a concert venue, and the initial attempt to get permission for Pavarotti to perform there was turned down by the local council. Just how far things have progressed since that 'no' can be gauged by the fact that the list of artists who have performed on the Twickenham concert stage includes heavy-metal outfit Iron Maiden. When architect Terry Ward designed the four new stands it was with only rugby in mind, and while preserving the noise generated by the fans was a factor in the planning, making sure 50,000 people could clearly hear Mick Jagger belting out 'Brown Sugar' was not.

Knight has spoken to many of the bands who have played at Twickenham, including Mike Rutherford from Genesis, and has been delighted to hear that the stadium acoustics have been given the thumbs up. 'I played in a charity golf day and partnered Mike Rutherford of Genesis and we talked about their shows at Twickenham, and he loves the venue because it is unique and intimate. The stadium was never designed with concerts in mind and it's a tribute to architect Terry Ward that the sound is so great. The only restriction we have on the stadium use is for concerts and when I started we asked the local council if we could have Pavarotti and they said no. Over the next ten years we did get agreement for three concerts a year at Twickenham of 50,000 capacity, and having managed them very carefully we can now do five concerts of up to 55,000 fans. We have seen the Rolling Stones, Rihanna, Iron Maiden and Lady Gaga, among others, perform on the stadium stage, which is built onto the pitch from the South Stand. The grass is covered for concerts to protect it, as fans stand on that area, and Keith Kent, the head groundsman, gets it quickly back to pristine condition. We do allow enough time for that to happen and it is a complex programming exercise. Keith was delighted he got to meet Mick Jagger at another Stones concert as he is a huge fan of the band.'

Knight's role at Twickenham is both challenging and illuminating, allowing him to see behind the scenes at both international rugby matches and music concerts involving some of the biggest names in the entertainment business.

The Rolling Stones put a snooker table into one of the dressing rooms while Mick Jagger, whose former home with Jerry Hall on Richmond Hill has an amazing view of the stadium across the Thames, requested shepherd's pie from the caterers and was seen on an exercise bike warming up for his performance. Lady Gaga transformed the changing room with the use of drapes and comfy chairs, and Knight said: 'The performers use the main changing rooms and they come in with their own production team. You wouldn't recognise the changing room and it was full of drapes and had a large wardrobe for all the costumes. We have to be very flexible to cater for all the demands of different usage.'

Since 1954, tens of thousands of Jehovah's witnesses assemble at Twickenham Stadium each summer for their annual convention. In the early years, a large swimming pool was erected in front of the West Stand for baptisms, with a walkway leading from the front of the terracing to the pool. A much smaller version is used nowadays during their three days at the stadium. Harold Clark, the first clerk of works at Twickenham, was a supporter of the annual convention because hundreds of women members of the church voluntarily cleaned his stadium after its use! In 2014 a world event for the church was staged at Twickenham, an arena that has witnessed many different uses since it was first built in the early 1900s. Not every application to the RFU to use the stadium is granted, despite the increasing need to maximise the use of the 82,000-seat arena.

One suggested attraction caused some concern as it involved a line of London buses being parked on the pitch.

Evel Knievel, the famous American stunt rider, broke his pelvis trying to leap over thirteen redundant single-decker AEC Merlin buses on 26 May 1975, in front of 90,000 people at Wembley. Despite his injury, a concussed Knievel addressed the crowd after the failed jump, announcing his retirement, and then walked out of the stadium before seeking treatment. Nevertheless, he returned to action five months later, successfully clearing fourteen buses in Ohio and setting a new world record. Knievel broke over 433 bones during his career, which earned him an entry in the *Guinness Book of World Records* as the survivor of 'most bones broken in a lifetime'. In tribute to his father, Knievel's son Robbie wanted to replicate the bus jump at Twickenham Stadium, but the RFU were not happy with the plans. The attempt was then scheduled for Wembley in 2009 but never took place.

The Twickenham car parks have featured stunt riders in the form of circus performers, with many famous circus touring companies using the large areas outside the stadium over the years. One of the less financially successful ideas for the west car park was formulated by Lieutenant-Colonel Dennis Morgan, assistant RFU secretary. He was keen to utilise the vast grass areas around the stadium on non-match days and came up with the idea of training lorry drivers. However, as Harold Clark revealed in his memoirs, there was a costly, fundamental error in Morgan's scheme. Clark explained:

Col. Morgan signed deal for the training of big wagon drivers in the west car park but the depth of the drains was too shallow. But contracts for £300 were signed and so the drains were replaced at a cost of £12,000 although no one knew – to save Morgan face.

Clark was also asked to look at the feasibility of building the RFU's own public house at the stadium – a concept that has mushroomed into sixty different bars and outlets for the sale and consumption of alcohol at the stadium in 2014. The idea of a single pub at Twickenham Stadium must have appeared a sensible way of generating revenue outside match days for the RFU in the 1960s, and the plans got as far as identifying the corner of Rugby Road and Whitton Road as the proposed site of a pub that would be called The Rugby Ball. Getting served on match days would have been a nightmare!

William Wavell Wakefield, 1st Baron Wakefield of Kendal, a former Harlequins and England player who became president of the Rugby Football Union in 1950, put his mind to maximising the use of the stadium, and his idea was to have a speedway track installed at Twickenham. Not surprisingly, like the pub, this project failed to come to anything, along with a number of others which would have certainly made Twickenham unique as a rugby venue. Harold Clark wrote: 'Sir Wavell Wakefield came up with the idea of removing the ring seats [bench seats in front of the terracing usually occupied by schoolchildren] and making a speedway track around the playing area and another idea was a supermarket on stilts in the north car park with parking underneath. Target golf was another idea that never happened.'

Francis Baron, the RFU chief executive, fought one of

his biggest committee battles over the commissioning of a statue designed to become the focal point of the South Stand development. It was designed by Gerald Laing and produced by his Scottish foundry to supplement the four rugby figures he had created in 1994 and stand atop the Rowland Hill Gates either side of the Golden Lion. Laing, a pop artist and sculptor, envisaged a line-out featuring five players; this has quickly become the most popular backdrop for supporters' photographs on first arrival at the stadium. It dominates the front of the South Stand and is purposely set into the ground, rather than on a plinth, to become more accessible to fans. However, the scheme nearly didn't get (27 feet) off the ground thanks to sustained opposition from RFU Council members. Baron, as we have seen, was used to this kind of reaction and was determined to plough on with the statue amid claims that it was the chief executive's folly and only intended to be his legacy to the sport.

Baron had heard all of the negative views and said: 'It was designed to be placed in that position on the South Stand piazza, but boy did I have a battle with certain council members over the statue. After we had already committed to having it constructed, certain council members tried to have it stopped because they felt the £700,000 cost should be distributed to the game. It's an absolutely bizarre argument when the whole South Stand development cost £140m and a key part was to have a wonderful entrance and only £700,000 was being spent to achieve it. We won that battle and even the people who were causing trouble at the time grudgingly accept it looks great.'

The statue was unveiled in June 2010 by Laing and it

would be his last major work before his death, aged seventy-five, a year later. 'Gerald Laing was able to unveil his last major work and it was so sad that he passed on so soon after it was completed. He has left us some iconic pieces and I believe the line-out was his finest work. The quality of the foundry work is superb and being able to walk through the sculpture is great – it's not on a plinth,' said Baron.

Engraved around the bottom of the statue are the five core values of the game of rugby union – teamwork, respect, enjoyment, discipline and sportsmanship – and John Owen, then president of the Rugby Football Union, commented at the unveiling: 'This is not art for art's sake but art for rugby's sake. We've dedicated it to the core values of our sport.' Laing's son Farquhar first offered his family's services to Twickenham in 1994, resulting in the 'Kicker', 'Winger', 'Scrum Half' and 'Forward' statues on the Rowland Hill Gates. The Laing family then set up Black Isle Bronze Ltd in Nairn in 2004, but Gerald moved into the Tite Street studios in Chelsea to produce the line-out. Seven months later he produced a half-sized line-out with the model mapped using a 3D scan-tech machine which got to an accuracy within 0.024mm. Then it was scaled up to twice life-size. Each part was cut out in pink Ureol, then made into moulds and heated to 1,150 degrees Celsius and the bronze poured in. There were sixty-six separate parts, which were then welded together and put on a lorry to travel from Inverness to Twickenham; it drew considerable attention from various police forces as it travelled almost the length of the country, being stopped three times to be inspected before being sent on its way to TW2.

After revealing his latest contribution to Twickenham, Gerald, who set up his first bronze foundry at Kinkell Castle on the Black Isle in 1978, said he chose to depict a line-out as it was a 'particularly dramatic' part of 'the most dramatic of games'. He then added, 'I thank the RFU for having the courage and conviction to commission this sculpture.' Architect Terry Ward was closely involved in the installation of the sculpture and even created 'grass' under the statue to complement the rugby action. 'We wanted people to be able to walk through and we had some Westmorland slate used and it's done in light and dark green to represent a pitch. I think it's fantastic. I wanted to make Twickenham a cultural arena and it became more of a community centre with sculptures; in the Live Room you can see a performance of *Les Miserables*, and they have concerts on the pitch now.'

How to 'dress' Twickenham's new stadium was a question put to Ward as the new look was created and, in what many will see as a suggestion that only confirms certain council members operate in a parallel universe, he was asked if ivy, similar to that crawling up the front of Wimbledon, was going to be added! Ward loves sculpture and, given a free hand, would have turned the outside of the stadium into a showcase for talent, but the only sculpture that actually hangs off the stands can be found attached to the back of the East Stand. It is a piece called 'Union', which was designed and produced by Tommy Steele, the singer and actor. He contacted the RFU and expressed his love of rugby and burning desire to give Twickenham a piece specifically created to encapsulate his enthusiasm for the sport. He already had two other sculptures on public display: 'Bermondsey Boy' at Rotherhithe Civic Centre and 'Eleanor Rigby', a tribute to the Beatles that he donated to the city of Liverpool. John Clark was at a meeting in which Steele presented his idea and also produced a small replica of the finished work. Clark remembers the meeting well and the unease the rest of the committee felt as Lee Angel, chairman of the ground committee, came into the room. 'Tommy Steele came to a meeting and brought a miniature of the sculpture. It was in the middle of the table and Lee came in a bit late and saw it and said, "Is that the Tommy Steele thing?" then, seeing the singer, quickly added, "Tommy, how are you?"'

Clark oversaw the repositioning of the Rowland Hill Gates to their present position, where they form a natural entrance to the West Stand, featuring the Golden Lion and the four Laing players. The move went smoothly, which made Clark slightly confused when he happened upon a tour party being shown around the grounds by one of the official guides. 'The four players were always going to go on the four pillars after we moved the Rowland Hill Gates, which features the lion, to its present position. I heard a tour guide talking to some visitors and he said the reason the team coach cannot come onto the concourse now is because when the gate was moved they made it too small. I saw him after the tour and said, "If the gate is too small now, how come all the bricks fit along with the gates?" Of course the team coach can come into the ground!'

The lion is the most striking of the statues on the Rowland Hill Gates, thanks to the gold that covers an animal that was locked away in a storage facility at the Lion Brewery for thirty years. 'I had the lion's gold leaf redone for the World Cup in 1991 and it's twenty-four carat gold. It should last around thirty years and its made of Coade stone,' said Clark. It was a gift to the RFU from Sir Desmond Plummer, chairman of the now extinct GLC, and an inscription below the lion reads: 'This lion made of Coade's artificial stone stood in front of the Lion Brewery, Lambeth, from 1837 to 1948 when the site was cleared for the building of the Royal Festival Hall. It was preserved – with the lion now standing on Westminster Bridge – at the express wish of King George VI. Presented on behalf of the Greater London Council to mark the centenary of the Rugby Football Union by Sir Desmond Plummer, Leader of the Council – April 1972.'

Art also features within the stadium, most notably in the form of a painting depicting a game in the late nineteenth century between Yorkshire and Lancashire (a copy of which I have in my home). The original hangs in the President's Suite on the third floor of the West Stand and features an intriguing mystery. The painting portrays a game between Yorkshire, in white, and Lancashire, in red-and-white hoops, played at Park Avenue, Bradford, on 25 November 1893 and was painted by William Barnes Wollen R.A. (1857–1936), a portrait painter who produced several rugby paintings along with a large number of specially commissioned war canvases. After he completed the rugby-match painting in 1895, it was hung in the Royal Academy in 1896 and then displayed in Leeds and Bradford. At this point it disappears from view, with the next sighting coming in a second-hand shop in Grey Street, Newcastle, in 1957. It was recognised by members of the Yorkshire RFU who paid £25 for it, and they presented it to Otley RFC. The Yorkshire club, which produced England captain Nigel Melville, retain ownership of the painting but have given it to the RFU for display.

The painting's unsolved mysteries have caused considerable debate, with one of the featured players, T.H. Dobson, not having actually played in the game. The faces of the referee, linesman and spectators have been replaced with RFU officials, including secretary George Rowland Hill and William Cail, who along with Billy Williams chose the site for Twickenham Stadium. However, the greatest debate is over a 'ghost' player whose existence was revealed when the RFU had the painting cleaned. A Yorkshire player was painted out of the picture, leading to suggestions that he was someone who opted to leave the union game and join the Northern Union, who had agreed to pay players.

Other attempts to bring colour and interest to what is, basically, a large concrete and steel bowl include special bricks placed in the ground just outside the west and north railings, featuring the names of some of the greatest ever England players, and blue plaques positioned at various points around the stadium carrying the names of players inducted since 2005 into the Twickenham Wall of Fame, which celebrates the best players from all over the rugby world who have played at the stadium.

Chapter Fourteen

Twickenham by numbers

When Paul Vaughan was appointed as business operations director of the RFU in 2000 he was given a clear idea of what was required. 'It was all about looking forward to the future and developing the assets they had and to deliver cash for the game.' That single quote, for many on the RFU Committee, summed up the problem with professionalism – it had turned the game into a money-making exercise, not the sport they had worked so hard as amateurs to help develop. Vaughan was helped in his role by having Baron in place as CEO. It would be Baron who would attract the ire of those within the Union who believed money-making ideas were contrary to the way the game should be run.

'Brian Baister was the chairman and Budge Rogers the president and I was interviewed by them along with Francis Baron. When I arrived the RFU turnover was £45m and when I finished in the commercial role in 2011 that figure had risen to £130m. I remember at the time of my interview being asked, "If you had a blank piece of paper, what would you do?" Among the things we talked about then were a hotel and more conference facilities. When I first joined we looked at the low-hanging fruit to drive finances – the television and sponsorship revenues. We wanted to change that into something that reflected the real value of Twickenham Stadium and the game. At that stage the old small South Stand was there along with the horseshoe shape of the new stands and the stadium was developing over time. The work that had been undertaken by Dudley Wood and Tony Hallett had carried the stadium and RFU to that point, but what happened when Francis arrived is that the whole operation was given real direction. It was a real privilege to be part of the team that was established at Twickenham.'

Just as the RFU had done when it first chose Twickenham as its home, the use of debentures continued to be a key element in the fundraising the Union needed to keep moving forward. Vaughan would also suggest a 'white market' for tickets that clubs did not need and that could be sold back to the Union at an agreed figure. 'The three new stands had been funded by debentures and we issued more as we went along and it was a very cheap way of raising capital. There are 15,000 debentures in the stadium. The way the tickets are distributed runs along the lines of 50 per cent plus one ticket going to the game through clubs and constituent bodies, and while debenture holders are part of the game, they don't get included in that figure going to the clubs. Clubs used to make money and keep themselves financially afloat by using their allocated tickets, which ended up all over the place. We brought those tickets back into the fold by agreeing to let clubs sell them to licensed hospitality outlets. I made a presentation to the RFU Council at the Hilton Hotel in London suggesting we explore a white market, with clubs selling unwanted tickets back to the Union who would on-sell them. Fran Cotton made an impassioned speech and that idea was crushed. I came back with another idea which was the official hospitality market – six operators would be licensed and be able to use the Red Rose logo. It was a compromise that came in just before the 2003 World Cup and then in the mid-2000s we really got our act together.'

The RFU formed the Twickenham Experience company in 2000 and holds 52.5 per cent of the shares in it; they received a cheque for £14m when it was set up. Vaughan is adamant this was good business and the benefits are still being seen, with this area of the operation providing an annual income bigger than gate receipts. 'Twickenham Experience paid £14m for the right to operate the hospitality at the stadium and that was a good deal to do at that time. Then there was only the room for hospitality in the North Stand, Invincibles in the East Stand plus the Obolensky and Wakefield restaurants. The double-decker tent in the north car park was created by Twickenham Experience. At that point the hospitality operating across the road from the East Stand – the Orchard – the one in the Cardinal Vaughan car park and Mike Burton's operation, along with various others, were unofficial. When we created the official hospitality scheme to place tickets that clubs wanted to get rid of, we offered those companies the chance to come on board. We gave them the use of the Red Rose, which they had to pay to get the license, and therefore clubs could sell tickets to these officially nominated operators. There were eventually six, including Events International, Mike Burton, National Sporting Club, Sportingclass, Tigers Events at Kneller Hall and another one who operated at the Masonic Lodge near Twickenham station.'

These significant developments were followed by the plans for the biggest change to Twickenham Stadium – the new South Stand. The building of a hotel and health club constituted new deals that had to be brokered and plans that needed to be passed by the authorities. However, gaining approval for these income streams was paramount for Baron and Vaughan, and they were committed to doing deals to ensure the plans became reality. Vaughan explained:

> The game went professional in 1995 and even now the sport is still coming to terms with that change. The game has to continue this transition and it may take another generation or even two before you become an effective model. Most sports in this country are run on the compromise of the amateur and the professional with principles that started in the Victorian era. The world has moved on but rugby, cricket and football are still structured in that county way and that is why you have various governance reviews. What has been

achieved at Twickenham to create this £150m business is by getting people to come with us on the journey, and it could have been achieved faster if it had been a commercially run operation. We brought in change by gaining the agreement of the people who were the fabric of the sport – amateur administrators who have come through the Union system. For about a hundred years there was gentle momentum in the game with the stadium evolving in a slow, ponderous way, and then we ramped it up over a twelve-year period and there was a lot of change for people to deal with.

Vaughan's first problem was to work out how many days a year Twickenham was used, and how to deliver a profit on a 75,000-seat stadium. 'However, that capacity was a mythical number because we only had 72,000 in the ground. You were looking at the Five/Six Nations internationals with the odd game in the autumn and so the number of matches at the stadium came down to around twenty a year and only ten filled the arena. It's not a great use of a sport's major asset. We had to generate more revenue and all the research indicated that there was a market for a hotel, a health club and conference/banqueting facilities in south-west London. Despite the transport issues, what we do have is a lot of parking space and people do want to come to the home of rugby. When I was looking at who would partner us, we ended up with Whitbread, my old employers, who had the Marriott franchise at that point, and we were in the middle of negotiations with them to come with us to manage the hotel off plan. They would bring in their expertise, reservation system and people. The RFU owns the hotel and Marriott manage it. We persuaded Virgin Active to change their model, which normally involves leasing a building, fitting it out and getting on with it. In this case it was very much a case of us buying everything and they brought their people and brand to the party. The don't have any capital investment at a club with 3,500 members and the two bits work together very well with hotel guests able to use what is a 40,000 square-foot gym.

'While we were in negotiations with Whitbread, they sold the franchise back to Marriott and so we had to deal with the Americans who were fantastic, accepting all that had been agreed. The conference/banqueting also works well together and is multipurpose. There were also pitch-side boxes as part of the hotel – there are six rooms that look out onto the pitch that are then turned into hospitality areas for matches. The original plan for the hotel had another floor, making it a 200-room facility, and we got nervous about that and so it was taken down to 156 rooms. We took a layer off and, in hindsight, they probably could have done with more rooms for the conference business. The cost of the development – originally £110m – had to go through the RFU Council and a committee was set up including members of the council who were surveyors and architects and it all worked out pretty well. It was funded by an extra thousand debentures, which was on top of the agreed limit of 15,000 for a temporary period. This wasn't a problem because we were increasing the capacity of the stadium to 82,000 and the extra debentures raised around £7m and we were very positive cash-wise and the rest – about £40m to £50m – came from our helpful bankers who knew we had a good cash flow from the stadium.

'This, of course, was anathema to an amateur game, with many voices asking the question, "Why are we spending this much on the stadium when we could be giving it to the game?" Our argument was simple; we told them that if we spent this money now to improve the facilities there would be even more money further down the line and that's exactly what has happened. It required a leap of faith to push this through and I fully understand that if you are the treasurer of a club at level six and know that a £500 grant from the RFU would put you back in profit then this kind of expenditure on Twickenham Stadium would become an emotional argument.'

With Twickenham Stadium facing substantial costs to become a complete bowl and to give southwest London a major hotel and leisure facility, the England team on the pitch started to falter following the success of the 2003 Rugby World Cup. Sir Clive Woodward departed having failed to get agreement from the Union for his vision of how the elite game in the country should progress, and successive coaches struggled to recapture winning ways. For Vaughan and his team, the pitches they were making to new and current sponsors had to be upbeat, despite those disappointing results. There was also the problem of the ongoing internal war between various factions in the Union and their opposition to Baron's vision, and the negative attitude to the RFU from Unions around the world – particularly among the other Home Unions who have consistently voted against the RFU on major issues.

'The World Cup win in 2003 was a step change for the financial side of Twickenham,' said Vaughan, 'although the problems – in terms of results – that followed the departure of Clive Woodward in 2004 did affect the commercial side. On the field always does. A losing team is a very diffi-cult sell to potential sponsors, while a Union washing its dirty laundry in public is another problem. If I was a sponsor, why would I want to sign up to partner a body that is a mess? Thankfully, you do have long-term commercial supporters who understand the benefit of staying with you. However, new sponsors do ask significant questions about what's happening within the Union. Undoubtedly we lost potential sponsors because of the negative publicity generated by the battle for control of the Union and that was also true in the period before I joined. If you look at the voting patterns of the Home Unions in recent times it really is a case of everyone against England, which probably reflects that the RFU hierarchy has come across as arrogant in the past. Rocking up with two coachloads of committee and wives compared to the one that is needed for the other Union when they come to us – the cost of that sort of thing is extraordinary.

'New Zealand understand the reality that they have the best team on the planet yet struggle to raise enough cash, so that means they have to come into the European market for sponsors and are reliant on playing extra Test matches up here that generate around a million pounds. It has gone up over the years and they do want a decent wedge and all the southern hemisphere teams are looking for that kind of boost to their earnings, which is why you see extra matches. Inevitably, England will generate the biggest revenue and

Twickenham Tests can deliver in the region of £5m to £6m, and when you add hospitality, TV [worth about £4m a game], sponsorship, plus food and drink the final figure is north of £13m and so it's not really that difficult to give away £1m to the opposition. During the 2011 World Cup, the NZRU had to try and increase by a considerable amount their gate takings, and tickets that would cost £40 for a normal All Blacks Test were suddenly £600 for the Cup final. I arrived in New Zealand halfway through the pool stages to find that they hadn't sold out the semi-finals or final at that point.'

Vaughan went on to comment on the perennial Twickenham problem of getting supporters to the ground. 'It would be interesting to extend the District line but the estimated cost is about a billion pounds to do that and so getting extra capacity into Twickenham railway station is the area to be improved. I cannot see the Underground option ever being taken up for what is a limited number of matches at Twickenham Stadium. If you were starting again with a national rugby stadium you would build it with better transport links. Another idea – a bit out of left field – would have been to relocate to the Olympic Stadium in Stratford, because you could keep the capacity at 80,000 and it has a massive amount of rail infrastructure. The only problem is that it isn't in Twickenham and that is the brand that has been created. In North America you don't have this kind of problem and you just relocate your franchise to a better area. There is an understandably strong emotional bond with Twickenham for the game, but if you were thinking it through and how things could work in the future, you would sell the land for redevelopment – it's a prime residential area – and move somewhere else!'

The Rugby Football Union is now based in open-plan offices in the new South Stand at Twickenham next to the Marriott Hotel, and the number of staff has increased to deal with the demands of a business that now generates more than £150m under chief executive Ian Ritchie. In 2013 the RFU employed 248 stadium, commercial and administration staff, with another 90 looking after the professional rugby side of the sport, plus 253 'in the field' engaged in rugby development. Wages and salaries for staff in 2013 came to £29.7m. When Twickenham has a full list of fixtures, involving four autumn internationals and three home games in the Six Nations, there is a substantial income from ticket sales, which in 2013 brought in £33.9m, but this is not the most lucrative of the RFU's income streams – hospitality and catering bank £37.5m. The Union owns 52.5 per cent of Twickenham Experience, the company created to maximise this financial windfall, which will continue to have a crucial role to play in generating funds for Twickenham's development and upkeep in the years ahead. Producing a successful product to display in one of the world's leading stadia is key to attracting other income, and in 2013 broadcasting contracts brought in £31.8m, ongoing sponsorship deals including on-pitch logos were worth £19.1m, while the various Twickenham retail shops and online business generated another £5.4m. Along with other revenues of £11m, the RFU was able to declare income of £153.5m in 2013, but it would be wrong to assume this is sitting in a bank account – the RFU spent £145.2m in the same financial period, with professional rugby in England getting £37.4m and rugby development for the wider game £26.3m.

Twickenham employs around 2,500 temporary staff on match days to service the lucrative hospitality operations that are dotted in and around the stadium and come under the umbrella of Twickenham Experience. The staff serve up to 9,000 meals for a sold-out match with fans paying, in some cases, £900 plus VAT for morning coffee, champagne reception, three-course lunch with wine, match ticket, 'free' bar, match programme, post-match tea, the chance to hear from players who took part in the match shortly after they have changed, and speeches from former greats. Just how much business is generated amid the eating, drinking and talking is impossible to gauge, but given the constant demand for hospitality places, Twickenham remains one of *the* corporate opportunities for major companies. Around the stadium on match days the 130 chefs operating in 32 different kitchens prepare 12,500 meals – there are 155 corporate boxes on top of the hospitality areas. Supporters milling around the ground are catered for by 36 fast-food outlets.

While those fortunate enough to be wined and dined are enjoying their sit-down meal, the rest of the stadium is queuing up for the many drinking opportunities now on offer at stadium. Incredibly, there are 58 different bars, 70 carts located at various points and 120 'hawkers' who walk around with small barrels of lager or beer on their backs, dispensing the liquid into plastic pint glasses they also carry. Why are there so many outlets? Well, the figures for alcohol consumption for the two Six Nations home matches at Twickenham in 2014 tell the story. At the Ireland game 48,323 pints of Beck's, 18,560 pints of IPA bitter, 4,048 pints of Strongbow cider and a staggering 89,616 pints of Guinness were bought, giving a total consumption of 160,547 pints – two for every fan in the ground. This did not include the bottled beers and lagers on offer in the hospitality areas. For the game with Wales there was an understandable drop in Guinness sales to 67,656, but an increase in IPA demand to 23,136 and an even bigger increase in lager, with Beck's pints up to 53,664, while 'only' 3,544 pints of Strongbow were sunk.

Given this considerable input of alcohol it is remarkable and probably unique to rugby that so little trouble occurs inside the stadium. The expansion of major bars has been needed to satisfy this substantial thirst, and the Scrum Bar at Twickenham is 47.5 metres long and has 40 staff to serve customers. They might be comforted to know the stadium features 134 toilet blocks!

While Twickenham prides itself on the range of ages of the fans who turn up for internationals, there are rules which affect some of the smallest fans. Babes in arms and children under two are only allowed into the stadium with the permission of the RFU. They do not require a valid ticket but will only be permitted into the lower tiers and enclosure areas. Children aged between two, and five are allowed in the stadium, provided they have a valid ticket and are seated in the lower tiers, while the upper tier of the stadium is deemed not suitable for children under eight and those who don't like to be up to a hundred-feet away from the pitch!

The Twickenham Marriott hotel has 156 rooms with six suites looking onto the pitch named after famous old players; these operate as normal rooms during non-match days but can be transformed into hospitality areas when required. The South Stand development benefitted from the RFU's assiduous purchase over many years of twenty-two houses that used to stand along Whitton Road, which were used by various staff members until they needed to be demolished to make way for the new development. The old South Stand terrace used to feature a clock, and this was replaced in 1950 by a weather vane featuring Hermes passing the ball to a rugby player through a set of posts. The vane has survived and can now be viewed – most easily from the West Stand upper levels – in its new position on the roof of the stadium in the southeast corner.

Notable firsts at Twickenham include 5 November 1988, when women were invited to an RFU reception for the first time for the match against Australia. Nowadays, the stadium features changing rooms for female match officials and stages women's internationals on the pitch. The programme for the first rugby international at Twickenham in 1910 cost just one penny. Identifying the players became easier in 1921 when the International Rugby Board introduced numbering on jerseys. In 1958, due to a supplier error, Wales had to play against England at Twickenham without the famous Welsh emblem, the Prince of Wales feathers on the left breast. The first souvenir programme for a Twickenham international was produced for the match with South Africa in January 1952 and was a shilling to purchase. The only time a feature has appeared in the match programme written by a player actually taking part in the game came in 1970. Ireland's Tony O'Reilly had retired from Test rugby in 1963 and wrote for the programme, only to be called up to play at the last minute when W.J. Brown of Malone dropped out. O'Reilly, who had already become a key figure in the Heinz company would go on to lead and become one of Ireland's most famous businessmen, wasn't even among the Ireland reserves. His amateur status was intact as he waived payment for the programme article.

One of the recurring problems that RFU officials have to deal with are the complaints from Twickenham residents fed up with rugby fans who have not been toilet-trained. The sight of a fan urinating against your wall or into your prized and neatly pruned hedge is guaranteed to trigger complaints to the Union. Police are not needed in or near the ground to control crowd behaviour – violent outbursts remain mainly on the pitch – and responsibility for ensuring fans do not trouble the neighbours falls to the security men employed by the RFU. Richard Knight, the Twickenham Stadium director, is responsible for ensuring match days pass off smoothly and that complaints are kept to a minimum. In a bid to tackle the recurring problem of fans caught short in the street – and around 1.2m head to Twickenham each year – Portaloos that cost the RFU more than £120,000 to hire have been installed in more than a dozen 'hot spot' locations.

Knight and the RFU are keenly aware that Twickenham Stadium is in a popular and crowded residential area rather than set among the quiet country lanes that existed when the RFU chose this setting in 1907. Patently, anyone who has moved to Twickenham since that date is well aware that they are setting up camp close to the home of English rugby, where tens of thousands of fans congregate on various Saturdays during the winter. Minimising the disruption caused by so many supporters and their cars has been a priority from the very early days of the stadium and continues to shape so much of the community work the RFU undertakes each year. The contact that now exists between the stadium owners and the local residents is in stark contrast to the 1980s, when the RFU was ex-directory and picking up the telephone to complain was not an option. Dudley Wood, who became secretary in 1986, changed that attitude: 'The local residents made a lot of complaints and now they could ring up. They also voiced their views in the local paper about what a nuisance the RFU was, but in nearly every case we were there before they had moved to Twickenham to live and so they must have noticed there was a stadium in their locality! We certainly tried to be good neighbours, clearing the streets after matches, putting in portable loos and offering tickets to local residents. We had a long-standing battle over the allotments and we did find places in other sites and we also gave them financial compensation but it was a long drawn-out process to move all of them from the north car park because we needed all the parking.'

Richard Knight accepts that maintaining a good relationship with the neighbours is a challenge, given the impact a sell-out 82,000 crowd makes for a very concentrated period of the day. There will always be complaints – they started in 1907 – and the RFU has to constantly interact to head off major problems. 'I believe we have been really responsible and have done a lot of work with the Concert and Match Day Group, which has representatives from local resident associations, local councillors from Richmond and Hounslow, and the police. I chair the group and the number of issues we have to solve is now pretty small. Fans urinating in the streets is something we are constantly trying to eradicate and we have ten to fifteen different areas where we install temporary toilets where we have identified hot spots. We make two hundred pairs of tickets for each international rugby match at the stadium available to residents in the local postcode areas and they are distributed by ballot. There are thirty-three free double-decker buses to help move fans to and from the stadium on match days and work is being undertaken at Twickenham station where the extended platforms can handle ten carriages rather than eight. We are continually looking at the transport situation and there is a lot of research work being undertaken around the 2015 Rugby World Cup, which includes the unique situation of dealing with Friday night matches.'

The nineteen concerts hosted at Twickenham Stadium between 2003 and 2013 saw more than 20,000 discounted tickets allocated to local residents, made available through the same ballot system that operates for international rugby matches. The RFU Local Residents' Ballot for the 200 pairs of international rugby tickets is open to anyone living in TW1, TW2, TW3 and TW7, with the application form found in the RFU's *Rugby Post* magazine delivered locally to 30,000 homes and businesses. The community magazine is produced three or four times a year and includes information about community relations with the RFU, ticket ballots and upcoming events. Twickenham Experience, the RFU's official hospitality operation, creates 2,500 temporary jobs each season to cater for the many dining and entertaining outlets that are in and around the stadium. The double-decker buses that take fans to and from Richmond and Hounslow to the stadium are free for two hours after the match finishes, with a 50p charge at other times.

'What fascinates me about Twickenham is the history of the place and how it has developed,' added Knight. 'It's more than just a stadium and is now an event experience – everything that is good about rugby happens here on a match day. It's not the most beautiful stadium in the world but there are not many better places to watch rugby or music concerts. New technology is very much part of the moving picture that is the stadium development. The guys who put the stands together didn't spend a huge amount of money yet put a great stadium together and our job is to respect the history while bringing it into the twenty-first century. The structure has come a hell of a long way – even in the ten years I have been involved – and we have developed the South Stand and it is now a genuine 365-day venue with twenty to thirty rugby games along with a lot of other activities.

'We have created a unique venue on non-rugby days. I was brought on board by Francis Baron and it was a new role because, previously, the stadium had been run by committee and it was time to modernise the structure when the game was going professional; the stadium was a bit of a sleeping giant at that time. We are using the stadium a lot more and the new Desso pitch means we can have more matches.'

For many local residents the 'face' of Twickenham is now provided by the yellow-jacketed stewards who look after traffic and public safety on match days. The police presence is moving closer and closer to Twickenham town centre, with the station an obvious focal point for their crowd-control work. Knight believes the stadium stewards working alongside the traditional honorary stewards, who show fans to their seats, is a successful melding of two types of crowd control. Honorary stewards used to have their own area for a pre-match meal under the old South Terrace, and many have long family associations with the stadium, helping to create a 'user friendly' atmosphere very similar to the positive vibe that exists at Wimbledon, where service personnel from the armed forces and civilian organisations like the fire service show ticket holders to their seats. 'We have a mix of honorary stewards, who look after the seating bowl, and also those who are paid to look after other areas. The total is around eight-hundred stewards. The majority of our matches do not have any police in the stadium except for a presence in the control box in the northwest of the stadium which keeps a close eye on traffic and crowd-control cameras; there are also St John's Ambulance and fire brigade representatives. Around 90 per cent of the traffic control outside the stadium is undertaken by us in liaison with the police. It used to be that if the police were inside the stadium grounds then we paid for them and if they were outside then it was their cost. Crowd behaviour doesn't warrant police inside Twickenham Stadium.'

Chapter Fifteen

The changing face of match day at Twickenham

The England players, who make the carefully choreographed walk from their special team coach which parks outside the West Stand gates at Twickenham, are, rightly, centre of attention on match days. It is in stark contrast to the attitude that pervaded the RFU not that long ago and ensured the players believed – particularly during the amateur era – that there was a 'them and us' scenario being played out. The committee areas were out of bounds to mere players. Now, the England luxury coach halts short of the gates on purpose, a move designed to create an avenue of fans to cheer the players all the way to their special 'Home' entrance at the base of the West Stand. The opposition have their own 'Away' doorway to reach their changing room. The walk to the changing rooms is designed to emphasise the fact that it is the players that 82,000 have turned up to watch, and everything is arranged to supplement this fact. Many will argue it is natural in a sport that is now professional for the players to be viewed differently, but a balance has to be found to ensure the England team remains accessible to the fans and does not exist in a bubble of self-importance. England's players are valued, revered by some, and treated correctly by the RFU; Stuart Lancaster, the head coach, has made it one of the pillars of his regime that those who wear the England jersey handle themselves in the right way. Respect earns respect.

Nothing epitomises the difference in attitude to England players at Twickenham on match days than the story Nigel Melville tells of the dreadful leg injury which ended his international career, against Ireland in 1988. Generations of England players had the distinct impression that the RFU men looking down from the committee box were doing just that – looking down on these chaps who had to be allowed to play even though many of them lacked the right school tie. Consideration for the players came down to individuals rather than a collective RFU effort to make the players feel they were a key element in the whole Twickenham experience. For Melville, the treatment he received that day was only magnified by the fact he was the England captain; while his team went on to register a significant 35–3 win over the Irish, with Chris Oti scoring a hat-trick (giving birth to the singing of 'Swing Low, Sweet Chariot'), Melville's tale is both sad and farcical, and all these years later still has the former scrum half shaking his head.

Melville is the CEO and president of rugby operations for USA Rugby and would never let one of his players be so badly treated as he was in 1988. He takes up the sorry tale. 'The rumour is that I hit the advertising hoarding that ran around the edge of the pitch on the West Stand side at Twickenham, but I think I landed just short. Either way, I dislocated my right ankle and broke a bone in my leg – ouch! I was carried from the field on a stretcher and then handed over to the St John's Ambulance guys who put me in an ambulance and drove me to the nearby West Middlesex Hospital where they transferred me to another stretcher and took me to the A&E – yes, still in full England kit! I was left lying on the stretcher in the queue waiting to be seen by a doctor – along with all kinds of people with sports injuries from their afternoon activities. I lay there for about thirty minutes and no one came to see me, my leg was now pretty painful and still dislocated. Then a nurse came to see me and asked if I was from "around here"? I explained I was from Yorkshire and so I had to fill some forms in. Then the nurse asked if I would donate my shirt as a raffle prize for the hospital. The RFU doctor, Ian Duff, arrived at the hospital, apologised for being late, and said it was an awesome second half and he just couldn't pull himself away! He then straightened my ankle and operated – I woke up in the orthopaedic ward.'

What happened next only serves to highlight how badly the RFU used to get its priorities wrong during the amateur days of the sport. With their national captain lying in an

NHS bed a short drive from the stadium, the RFU sent along two members of the committee. They found Melville in his bed and, with crass insensitivity, proceeded to tell him that he would not be able to take out an insurance claim against the RFU as he did not collide with either the advertising boards or the wall around the pitch. Melville was stunned by their attitude and to this day cannot believe that was the message they brought to the hospital bed of the injured England captain. 'The next day I was visited by two RFU guys who told me that I hadn't hit the wall that ran around the pitch and I would not have a claim against them! I then discharged myself from the hospital and went to a private hospital to get the next operation done. Basically, even if you were the England captain in 1988, if you got injured at Twickenham, the RFU just sent you to casualty like everyone else.'

When England won 9–8 against Wales in 1980 in one of the most violent matches ever staged at Twickenham, there was an explosion of euphoria from the supporters, who swarmed onto the sacred turf. The victory kept England on course for the Grand Slam, which they would clinch at Murrayfield against Scotland. Faced with thousands of fans on the pitch and having little chance of dispersing them, RFU secretary Bob Weighill had to do something. Recognising that the crowd was singing for Bill Beaumont, the victorious England captain, he used the stairs that linked the committee room with the tunnel area, opened the latched gate and entered the England changing room. The players were still coming to terms with the ferocity of a match that had seen Wales flanker Paul Ringer sent off for a late tackle on England outside-half John Horton. That incident set the tone for the rest of the match and Welsh fans took the defeat so badly that ties were printed in Wales just days later which had the score shown with 'two tries to nil' in an attempt to claim a moral victory for the fourteen Welsh players beaten by three Dusty Hare penalties. Beaumont was dumbfounded to be asked to go out and respond to the crowd. It had never happened in his career to date and the RFU had no established protocol for 'this sort of thing'. Egged on by Weighill, who could see his beloved pitch being trampled by the hordes, Beaumont agreed to follow the secretary up the committee stairs and to appear in front of the Royal Box.

Beaumont recalled: 'The 1980 match against Wales wasn't a great spectacle and it was a different game. It was one of those things. We knew we had a chance of doing something as a team and it was like going into the Coliseum. At the end of the game the crowd invaded the pitch and not many of them will have seen us beat Wales before – it was the only time I defeated Wales in my playing career. I was in the changing room and while we were relieved, everyone was knackered because it was a tough old game. Then Bob Weighill came in and said the crowd was chanting my name and he asked if I would go up to the committee box and acknowledge the crowd. It was the only time in my career I did that and I stood there with the crowd cheering. I thought, "What do I do now?" I didn't know if I should wave or clench my fists and ended up giving them a pathetic double thumbs up.'

Before that momentous match, Beaumont had under-taken the normal pre-match routine of walking around the pitch in his England blazer, waving to the crowd, hearing the banter and even signing a few autographs. Beaumont also took his place for the traditional photograph with the North Stand in the background, a practice that many feel is sadly missing from the current game. While you can argue that the sheer number of matches players get to play in for their country would mean filling up an entire wall in their home with pictorial mementos of each cap, there was something special about the teams announcing themselves to the crowd by taking their seats or standing for the official photograph. They usually took place twenty minutes before kick-off, with the players returning to the dressing room for a final cigarette or chat. Before the advent of sponsored jerseys and copious amounts of kit, those lucky enough to be in the England XV entered the dressing room where a numbered jersey was waiting along with socks and a track-suit. The player supplied his own shorts and boots. If you were a replacement and didn't play, the jersey had to be handed back along with the socks and tracksuit – as well as the rug they were given to ward off the cold on the touch-line. Today, players have two jerseys so they can change into a new one at half-time. They are also made of breath-able lightweight material, until like the heavy cotton that Beaumont had to deal with.

There has also been a radical change to the balls used for Twickenham internationals and around the rugby world. Gilbert used to supply their famous leather match ball for England home games, with two being blown up specially for every contest. Most other grounds made three available, but Twickenham only used two, with the other on hand in case something happened to the first, which the crowd were always quick to throw back to keep the game going. One ball did go missing during a match with Wales in 1960, with a quick-thinking visitor deflating the prize to smuggle out and then reinflating it again when he got home to put on display. It was seen by a local police officer who, according to Wallace Reyburn in his history of Twickenham, returned it to HQ; no charges were made. In those days the two balls became the property of the respective captains after each match. Now, half a dozen balls are spread around ball boys, with the Gilbert company having developed new types of materials to keep their name associated with the sport.

Beaumont and the players of yesteryear shake their heads in amazement as they watch England internationals of today on the pitch before an international match in their training tops, going through fitness and warm-up routines that would have left players of previous eras absolutely shattered before the game kicked off. The kickers go through practice for line kicks, up-and-unders and endless shots at the posts from the most oblique angles. In 1980, Dusty Hare would practise a few kicks while his fellow Leicester team-mate Clive Woodward would try to catch the ball behind the posts by leaning forward and taking it on the full with his hands behind his back! Beaumont added, 'When I played, you arrived on match day with the England team at around 2 p.m. and walked around on the pitch, signed a few autographs and there was nothing like the warming up they do now with cones and lots of balls. We would have been knackered doing the warming up they go through. After the game, you would go to the tea room, and getting tickets for tea was the real prize. You got two complimentary tickets for the match you were playing in and were allowed to buy four more. The most popular guy was Richard Ankerson, the ticket officer, and he would always try and help the players out; now he is, quite rightly, a privileged member who receives two committee area tickets for each match. For me, Twickenham on a match day has a special feel. What always made it feel like home was standing in my kit on the pitch before the kick-off singing the national anthem.'

Enormous thought and preparation goes into the match-day 'experience', with Twickenham laying on music and various displays by the armed forces, such as abseiling down from the roof to the pitch. Giant flags of the competing nations are laid out on the grass, the traditional band plays and now opera singers add their voice to the national anthems. There are half-time interviews with former players and replays of the best bits of the first half, along with adverts sent spinning around the perimeter hoardings at two different levels, thanks to the new technology that has been installed at the stadium. There was disquiet when Twickenham agreed to allow advertising hoardings at the ground in the early 1970s and those painted versions – which cost £5,000 per season to have installed – have given way to hi-tech, state-of-the-art explosions of sight and sound, backed up by logos painted onto the pitch and blaring out from post protectors.

Most importantly, for the players who face an increasingly dangerous game in which car-crash style injuries are all too common, the changing area contains a fully equipped medical room that can offer on-the-spot treatment before a player – if necessary – is sent to hospital. He will be accompanied by members of the team's medical staff and management and certainly not left to fend for himself as Melville was in 1988. Many question the number of changes that Twickenham has enthusiastically embraced, but the improved medical care and attention for injured players is one area where they can justly feel proud.

Outside the hi-tech ground, it appears as though every piece of land and free space around Twickenham is utilised as plots for temporary hospitality facilities, which only highlights the continuing problem with the site – it's not big enough. The playing fields and playground at the Chase Bridge and the Cardinal Vaughan schools, the car park of a self-storage unit which becomes the 'Orchard Enclosure' for the duration of the games, and the cricket pitch at Kneller Hall (the Royal Military School of Music) all become homes to marquees and armies of staff delivering three-course meals and fine wines. They are needed because the on-site operations are full to bursting; with the stadium work completed, this situation will persist for years to come or until demand wanes. What the RFU are planning for Twickenham is a comprehensive upgrade to ensure the 2015 Rugby World Cup has a state-of-the-art arena. This involves expenditure of £76m to install, among other things, new LED floodlighting and a full IT 'backbone', as Richard Knight likes to describe the improvements. He said: 'We are modernising the stadium using hi-definition Wi-Fi, which will allow fans to upload and download information to add to the match-day experience for 82,000 people. We are putting in video-board screens that will hang off the front-edge stadium roof at the north and south ends to replace the existing screens that are seven years old. Technology now allows you to do this because materials are so much lighter. That will allow us to put in another 650 seats, which is great. Ticketless entry to the stadium is getting close to becoming a reality. In the future supporters could gain access by swiping bar codes from their mobile phones.'

Knight has introduced LED screens that send sponsors' messages, and also those from fans, speeding around the entire stadium in an explosion of light. Sophie Goldschmidt, the RFU's chief commercial officer, told the *Daily Telegraph* that fans may in future be able to order drinks to their seats using their mobile phones. 'At the minute it is pretty hard to make a phone call or send a text on match days,' said Goldschmidt. 'Most people now want to watch highlights on their mobiles or send videos or pictures and high density will allow that. Thirty to forty per cent of the stadium will be able upload serious amounts of data at the same time.' The stadium is also being given HD Wi-Fi that will allow the RFU to increase its communication with supporters via social media such as Twitter and Facebook on match days. 'Going digital has been a big focus for us,' she added. 'It is how we are communicating with our current and new fans. We now have greater access to our players, giving us more unique content. On match days, we want to push that out to supporters via their mobiles.'

This is only a snapshot of what is being planned, but one thing is for certain; no matter what changes occur at the stadium, barring the installation of a tunnel under the three roundabouts that form natural traffic choke points from a point close to Twickenham Stadium up to the bridge over the

Thames, the car transport situation is not going to be solved any time soon. The Underground will not be extended to take in a stadium stop, which leaves Twickenham station as the only aspect of the travelling experience that might be improved in the coming decades. Of course, they could move the stadium to a site with excellent transport facilities, but rugby doesn't do logic. The Millennium Stadium was built on the same city-centre site in Cardiff that housed the old arena, and Lansdowne Road was given a major facelift (and renamed the Aviva Stadium for sponsorship purposes) on the same patch of ground in Ballsbridge in a residential area of Dublin, even though keeping it there severely restricted the amount of seating that could be installed. Twickenham is English rugby and English rugby lives in Twickenham. That is how it's been since 1907 and that is how it will be in the future.

Sources

Cooper, Ian, *Immortal Harlequin: The Story of Adrian Stoop*, The History Press, 2004

FitzSimons, Peter, *Nick Farr-Jones: The Authorised Biography*, Hutchinson, 1993

Harris, Ed, *Twickenham: The History of the Cathedral of Rugby*, Sportsbooks, 2005

Reyburn, Wallace, *Twickenham: The Story of a Rugby Ground*, George Allen & Unwin, 1976

Warner, Philip, *The Harlequins: 125 years of Rugby Football*, Breedon Books, 1991

Woodward, Clive, *Winning!*, Hodder, 2004

Acknowledgements

This book would not have been possible without the help and support of so many people. My thanks go to Iain MacGregor and the staff at Aurum Publishing for coming up with the idea and their help in bringing the book to life, in particular copy-editor Ian Allen. To my wife, Alex, and children, Tom and Jess, this would not have been possible without your patience and understanding. My thanks also go to those who generously gave up their time to help provide the memories that make up this book: Richard Ankerson, Francis Baron, Bill Beaumont, Will Chignell (RFU head of communications), John Clark, Lawrence Dallaglio, Paul Davies, Peter Hain MP, Michael Heal (journalist and former Oxford blue), Tony Hallett, Colin Herridge, Keith Kent, Richard Knight, Stuart Lancaster, Nigel Melville, Brian Moore, Pat Murphy, Michael Rowe and his staff at the World Rugby Museum, Paul Vaughan, Terry Ward (Ward McHugh Associates) and Dudley Wood. Also of invaluable help has been: the forensically researched work of Ed Harris in his book *Twickenham, the History of the Cathedral of Rugby*; the window on a bygone era of rugby provided by Wallace Reyburn in *Twickenham: The Story of a Rugby Ground*; and the pages of the *Richmond and Twickenham Times*.

Index

INDEX

INDEX